THE WATERFORD REBELS OF 1849

The Last Young Irelanders and their Lives in America, Bermuda and Van Diemen's Land

Brendan Kiely

GEOGRAPHY PUBLICATIONS

Published in Ireland by
Geography Publications,
Kennington Road
Templeogue Dublin 6W

ISBN 0 906602 61 0

Cover Design by Bernadette Kiely and incorporates detail of her painting 'Land'
(48'' x 60'', oil on board) which is one of a series made for 'Famine', an
exhibition originated by the George Moore Society, Claremorris, Co. Mayo
which toured Ireland, U.S.A. and Canada in 1995/1996.

Printed by Litho Press Co., Midleton, Co. Cork, Ireland.

CONTENTS

DO MO MHUINTIR

An Gorta

'45 Da dhubhadar
'46 Ní raibh ceann ann
'47 Board of Works
'48 Smith O'Brien
'49 Row Cheapach Choinn
(ó m'athair Dónall Ó Cadhla)

PREFACE

1849 is the second part of a trilogy, which began with *The Connerys The Making of a Waterford Legend*. The common themes are the relationship between Ireland and Australia, transportation and the penal system, opposition to the Union of Ireland with Great Britain and the declining influence of Irish speakers on the course of Irish history..

This work also draws heavily on Irish folklore and sources in the Irish language and seeks to emphasize their importance in any attempt to understand events in the first half of nineteenth century Ireland. Indeed it is hoped that that the book will demonstrate that the Young Ireland Rising of 1849 was the last occasion when an Irish speaking "army" took the field.

In keeping with an emphasis on the lower strata of Irish society a great deal of biographical detail is included in the Appendices particularly regarding prisoners and emigrants. Young Ireland was as much a literary as a revolutionary movement so poetry is not neglected either. Its style may be difficult to appreciate for those used to contemporary verse but remember it must be judged on the standards of its own day. The book also attempts to give some new insights on the history of Bermuda, the development of Tasmania in the nineteenth century and Irish revolutionary movements in the United States.

In offering an original five line history of the Great Famine, which combines Irish and English the book lays claim to having the shortest history of *An Gorta* but no less perceptive for that. Economy of words also pervades a more general treatment of this topic but there is no scarcity of insights.

Finally, the trilogy is deeply concerned with exploring the inability of 'English' law as represented by the statutes, judges, magistrates, courts and police to gain the same acceptance as the common law of the Irish peasantry particularly in those upland communities who in 1848 and 1849 were willing to follow the Green Flag.

ACKNOWLEDGEMENTS

I am deeply grateful to Dr. John B. O'Brien for his assistance over many years. His untimely death is a great loss to the study of Australian history in the south of Ireland. I would also like to thank Professor John A. Murphy who kindly read the script. During the years of research the staff of the following institutions were always courteous and helpful: the Cork City Library, the National Library of Ireland, the National Archives Dublin, the Royal Irish Academy Library, the Library and Department of Irish Folklore University College Dublin, the British Library, the Public Records Office in Kew, the Archives Office and State Library of New South Wales, the Mitchell Library Sydney, the Archives Office and State Library of Tasmania, and finally the Library of Congress and the Archives of the Catholic University of America in Washington D.C.

In Cappoquin I got very useful information from the late John Green of Castle St., the late James Crotty of Lr. Main St., Mr. Thomas McCarthy of Barrack St. and Mrs. Helen McGrath of Drumroe. I am also obliged to Mr. Tony McCarthy who generously made available his survey of Old Affane graveyard and his research on Hugh Collender. Fuair mé eolas freisin o'n Dr. Pádraig Ó Macháin agus o'n Dr. Diarmuid Ó Mathúna. I am similarly indebted to all those people I met around Longwood, Co. Meath on a fine summer's day in 1996. My thanks to Mr. David Whelan of Glencairn, Lismore for producing the maps. Mention must also be made of the historian Anthony Breen of Suffolk who kindly sent me some research completed after the publication of his own study on the Rising of 1849. Thanks are also due to the historian and researcher Ms. Dianne M. Snowden of Richmond, Tasmania who traced material on John Shea. Similarly, I have not forgotten the hospitality of Dr. Marian Sheehan and Mr. Peter Collins of Sydney and Ms. Marianne and Professor Richard Davis of Hobart. I would like to thank the Sisters of the Josephite community and Mr. John Dance of Cygnet and Mr. Damien Bester of the *Derwent Valley Gazette,* New Norfolk, Tasmania. I also owe a great deal to Ms. Donna Barry and Mr. Michael J. Moriarty.

The work would never be completed without the support of my own family especially my mother Alice. However, Rita, Ann, Patrick & Deirdre, Joseph & Lynn and Dónall will all be glad it is finished. Faraor tá m'athair Dónall, a col ceathrar Dónall agus a ghaol Pluincéid Brunnoc ar slí na fhírinne anois ach tá a mbéaloideas beo agus istigh sa leabhar seo.

Táim buíoch do mo fostaitheoirí, An Roinn Gnóthaí Soisialacha, Pobail agus Teaghlaigh a thug an t-ám dom dul go dtí an Astráil chun an taighde a dheanamh agus níos deanaí sos chun an leabhar a scríobh. Gabhaim buíochas freisin do Tomás Caomhánach agus do Cumann Fhorbairte Ceapach Choinn a thug an cúnamh chun an leabhar seo a fhoilsiú.

ABBREVIATIONS

A.D.B.	Australian Dictionary of Biography
Adm.	Admiralty Papers
A.O.N.S.W.	Archives Office of New South Wales
A.O.T.	Archives Office of Tasmania
C.C.	Catholic Curate
C.O.	Colonial Office
Co.	County
Con.	Convict Papers
Conn.	Connecticut
C.R.F.	Convict Reference Files
C.S.O.	Chief Secretary's Office
D.C.	District of Columbia
G.P.O.	General Prisons Office
H.O.	Home Office
Ill.	Illinois
Imp. Bay	Impression Bay
Kk.	Kilkenny
Ky.	Kerry
L.S.D.	Land Survey Department
Mass.	Massachusetts
Mont.	Montana
M.P.	Member of Parliament
N.A.	National Archives Dublin
N.L.I.	National Library of Ireland
N.S.W.	New South Wales
N.Y.	New York
O.P.	Outrages Papers
P.P.	Parish Priest
P.R.O.	Public Records Office Kew
Prot.	Protestant
R.C.	Roman Catholic
R.M.	Resident Magistrate
Tas.	Tasmania
Tipp.	Tipperary
Wat.	Waterford
V.D.L.	Van Diemen's Land
Vic.	Victoria
Vt.	Vermont

FIGURES

INTRODUCTION

It is a long time ago since my father told the story of an ancestor that fought for Ireland at Cappoquin in 1849. The day was wet, he was late, the other rebels had left their meeting place but he still set out for Cappoquin. It was dark when he reached the outskirts of the town and learned that the attack on the barracks had failed. He took shelter in an outhouse and when he awoke in the morning he discovered he was in a hen house. He immediately returned to his home covering the ten miles to Sliabh gCua in Waterford's high country, in record time. My father also had a rhyme in Irish and English, which distilled the story of the Great Famine to just five lines, the last being Cappoquin and 1849.

From other relatives in the same Irish-speaking tradition came the story of the rebel Paddy Larry Walsh and how a kindly policeman allowed him to escape to America. The memoirs of Séamas Ó Caoimh from Melleray in the Knockmealdown mountains whose granduncle was at Cappoquin in 1849 gave another insight from the Irish folklore of Sliabh gCua on the event.

In the town itself the story of a man searching for a midwife for his pregnant wife and trying to avoid both rebels and police was still remembered by their descendants. Similarly, a relative of Michael Cavanagh, poet, writer and revolutionary, was able to point out the house in which he lived. Most townspeople are aware that something happened there in 1849 but not too sure on the exact details.

In the following pages you will learn all about the Young Ireland Rising of 1849 and its significance in Irish history. Its leaders were modern men well versed in nationalism and republicanism but the rank and file rebels were very much of Old Ireland – lovers of the factions and men and women who would follow a Gaelic chieftain. It was also the last time for an Irish-speaking "army" to take the field and defeat had serious consequences for the future of that language. The failure of 1849 sent another wave of Irish political emigrés to the United States and penal exiles to Bermuda and Van Diemen's Land. The lives of these rebels abroad form an important part of the story of 1849.

It is useful to begin with the best known Young Ireland rising that of
1848. On 29 July 1848 a large force of heavily-armed Tipperary
constabulary were beseiged by a rebel force, led by William Smith
O'Brien, at the Widow McCormack's house at Farrenrory near
Ballingarry. The police refused to surrender safe in the knowledge that
the Widow's spacious, well-built, two story, slated house which
dominated a garden enclosed by a perimeter wall was a better defensive
position than most barracks. The rebels had no time to begin a formal
siege as they knew the British army and police re-inforcements were on
the way. Poorly armed and without artillery they decided on a frontal
assault with inevitable results. After some casualties the attack was
broken off. Most of the leaders including Smith O'Brien were soon
captured but even so the harvest witnessed a Second rising.

In September John O'Mahony was the overall commander. His plan was
to take Carrick-on-Suir in a simultaneous two pronged assault from north
and south of the river Suir. It required the rebels to capture all the police
barracks in these areas and also to prevent the British army from
advancing quickly from Waterford City. This could be achieved by
destroying the bridge at Grannagh and cutting the city's road link with
South Kilkenny. Similary, to prevent any military advance along the south
bank of the Suir the rebels needed to hold the town of Portlaw on the main
road from Carrick to Waterford.

O'Mahony's northern division began well when they burned the police
barracks at Ahenny (also know as the Slate Quarries) but they failed to
overrun Glenbower barracks and after their repulse here they did not
press on to Carrick. In South Kilkenny the rebels failed to destroy
Grannagh bridge and were unable to take Kilmacow barracks. Similarly,
Portlaw barracks did not fall to O'Mahony's southern division and while
a small raid for privately held arms was successful near Rathgormack an
attempt to seize a clergyman's arsenal near Mothel failed. The book
opens with O'Mahony's defeated southern division, which have returned
to their base and are about to disperse.

AHENNY HILL
SHOWING THE CONSTABULARY BARRACK DESTROYED BY THE INSURGENTS, 1848

CHAPTER 1 INSURRECTION

On Friday, 14 September 1848 the Green Flag flew on Cruachán Paorach, the high hill which dominates the town of Kilmacthomas in East Waterford. However, when the military and police arrived, the rebels had vanished like a Comeragh mist.[1] John O'Mahony's ambitious barracks campaign was over and the Second rising of 1848 had failed. The loyalty and discipline of the Irish police, which had repulsed the forces under William Smith O'Brien M.P., at Farrenrory on 29 July, had not diminished with the passing of six weeks. The rebel muster on the slopes of Cruachán Paorach ended a trinity of failure, which began with the debacle at the Widow McCormack's and includes the abortive Chartist/Confederate coup at London on 16 August. Now, it appeared that armed resistance to the Crown and the Union was over – yet barely one year would elapse before part of the South of Ireland was once more in revolt.

Despite a reward of £100 and concentrated sweeps and searches of the countryside around Carrick-on-Suir, John O'Mahony eluded the authorities. Although a fugitive he continued to organise a secret revolutionary organisation and had some success in the high country of County Waterford. Similarly, he did not neglect his ties with faction leaders in the uplands of South Tipperary and South Kilkenny. He was helped in this work by Philip Gray, who had been one of his main commanders in the September rising. In January 1849 O'Mahony escaped to Wales on board the Dungarvan Schooner *Johanna,* and soon made his way to Paris.[2] Gray alone remained, the last Young Irelander in the field, his belief in the ultimate success of the revolution undiminished. This fervour sustained him through a harsh winter, much of which he apparently spent in the open with only the odd respite of the shade and heat of a limekiln or a bed in a friendly house. Yet his energy and perseverance enabled the secret organisation to grow. He also benefited from an elaborate American alibi in which Thomas Devin Reilly's newspaper the *Citizen* announced his safe arrival in New York, en route to the American West.[3]

In 1848 the Suspension of the Habeas Corpus Act proved a most effective weapon for the government allowing it to intern without trial most of Young Ireland's middle-ranking leadership. However, once the authorities were satisfied that the movement was defeated the releases began. James Fintan Lalor, the radical advocate of land reform, was discharged from Newgate Gaol, Dublin in November 1848 his release speeded by ill health. Joseph Brenan, journalist and radical revolutionary, was released in the last batch of prisoners from Kilmainham Gaol in March 1849.[4] These two, together with Thomas Clarke Luby, a Dublin law student, who somehow avoided the attention of the authorities in July/August 1848 and Philip Gray would be the main figures in the 1849 movement. It was they who organised a revolution for Sunday 16 September 1849. This date has special significance in Irish history for not alone was it Young Ireland's last battle but it also marks the end of Old Ireland.

When Daniel O'Connell spoke at the great mass meeting, on the Hill of Tara, in August 1843, he was at the height of his power. Not alone was he the leader of Old Ireland but he had attracted around him a gifted group of young men and women who enthusiastically supported his pursuit of repeal of the Union. This group who later became known as Young Ireland had grown up with Catholic Emancipation and with the gains made by Irish Catholics as regards access to public office during the Liberal government of 1835 to 1841. The Young Irelanders, with their cultural and romantic nationalism, most attractively, seductively and passionately espoused in the *Nation*, were also in the forefront of modern European political thought so their expectations were further increased – and O'Connell could not deliver. Sir Robert Peel, the Tory Prime Minister and his old enemy effectively ended the Repeal campaign by banning the mass meeting organised for Clontarf in October 1843. More disillusionment set in when Peel established the Queen's Colleges at Cork, Galway and Belfast. The Young Irelanders wished the new colleges to be non-denominational but O'Connell following episcopal dictat, favoured a Catholic ethos for Cork and Galway and a Presbyterian ethos for Belfast. The split finally came in the summer of 1846, as the Tories left office to be replaced by a Liberal government under Lord John

DANIEL O'CONNELL

Russell. The Young Irelanders were unwilling to endorse O'Connell's absolute commitment to the principle of non-violence.

This happened as the countryside was in turmoil – that wonderful plant from the Andean highlands, the potato, was stricken and all Ireland was laid low.

The critics of the Irish peasantry – and there were many – charged that they were a lazy, immoral and violent lot. But there was nothing soft about cultivating potatoes whether it was the making of the ridges, the application of manure, the putting of clay to the potatoes, the digging of the tubers not to mention their picking. A day, with a *grafán,*[5] in a high field was far from easy.

When the blight struck first, in the autumn of 1845, the poorest people barely clung on. In 1846 *'Ní raibh ceann ann'* – there wasn't a potato to be had.[6] Now, the poor cottiers, the labourers and farmers big and small had lost their main source of food. For the cottiers and labourers the disaster was total for their very existence depended on the money earned from harvesting and setting *other* peoples' potatoes. It was this money together with that from cutting hay and corn, which paid the rent for their little gardens. A small farmer would have more capital but he would still have to find a new source of food and that meant money. Even a strong farmer would have to draw on other resources. Moreover, the "pig in the parlour" - that great friend of the Irish poor – could no longer be fattened since where was the money to come from to buy grain now that there were no potatoes. An Irish economy underpinned by the potato, began to contract and in some rural areas tottered on the verge of collapse.

Thus began a cycle of starvation, disease, evictions and emigration, which lasted well into 1849. Indeed it could well be argued that, like a biblical plague, the immediate effects lasted the whole seven years to 1852. Some sought refuge in the new workhouses, others tried to survive on the public works and those who could afford it left for England, Scotland, Wales, America or Australia.

Hunger and ruin made people desperate. The British government's response was an old one – repression. In 1846 the 1st Royal Dragoons clattered into action against the poor at Dungarvan as they attempted to seize food supplies. Local taxation, in the form of escalating poor rates, drove even respectable farmers to adopt the tactics of *Na Buachaillí Bána*. Spiralling violence was barely contained by the bailiffs, the British army, the constabulary, the courts and penal system and the conditions which engendered it barely ameliorated by the various relief agencies, the Poor Law Guardians and the Commissioners for Public Works. It was in such a climate that the Young Irelanders set up the Irish Confederation on 13 January 1847.

Daniel O'Connell, an old man and in poor health, now faced the most serious challenge to his almost 20 year leadership of the Irish popular party. During this time he had seen off many ambitious Irish Catholic rivals but he now faced a determined group who quickly established affiliated clubs all over Ireland. In May 1847, as Old Ireland, his Ireland, tottered under the weight of famine and disease O'Connell died at Genoa. His son, John, was unable to fill the power-vacuum, which followed the loss of the great leader.

The French Revolution of 1848 left a deep impression across the continent and soon Europe was ablaze from the Atlantic Ocean to the Ural Mountains. The Young Irelanders believed their hour had come. Joseph Brenan, a young Cork poet drafted the following resolution of the Desmond Club:

> That the only means by which advantage can be taken of the opportunity which late events on the Continent of Europe have presented to the Irish people for the achievement of their rights from an unwilling and hostile government are the termination of existing divisions and the combination of all Irishmen in one great national alliance for the assertion of Ireland's independence.[7]

Soon a delegation from the Irish Confederation led by William Smith O'Brien was in Paris, seeking help from the new French Government but the latter was unwilling to draw the wrath of England on its infant regime.

Dublin Castle quickly cracked down on its Irish revolutionaries. Under the new Treason-Felony Act they arrested John Mitchel and secured his conviction and transportation. It was only a matter of time before the rest of the Young Irelanders would join him in involuntary exile. The Dublin Confederate Clubs met in crisis session to decide on a response. Joseph Brenan, who had written for Mitchel's newspaper the *United Irishman* and was now writing for its successor the *Irish Felon,* argued passionately that the movement should strike immediately and attempt to seize the initiative from the government. However the policy adopted was one of concealing arms and passive resistance. This decision exasperated Bob Ward, a saddler from South Kilkenny, who declared; 'Not yet sufficiently prepared! There are some people who will never be prepared – fellows who, - if the Almighty rained down rifles ready loaded from Heaven, - would ask Him to send down Angels to pick them up and fire them'.[8]

William Smith O'Brien and the leaders left for the southeast and set in train a chain of events which ended in defeat outside the Widow McCormack's house. Many of the leaders had been under the delusion that the year was 1798 and that at least a few of the Catholic clergy of Waterford and Lismore, Ferns, Ossory and Cashel and Emly would rally their flocks to the rebel standard. In fact, nearly all the priests still revered O'Connell and anyway they took the pragmatic view that Ireland had suffered enough without putting the country through the horrors of war.

On top of this the Young Irelanders were very poor military men. Smith O'Brien was unable to command the men of Munster as well as his ancestor Brian Boru. The only person to make any headway against government forces was John O'Mahony and thereby illustrated the great irony that no matter how much the 1848 leadership called on the people of Ireland for support, it was only in the main Irish speakers, the men from the high country of Waterford, Tipperary and Kilkenny, the men who loved the factions that would follow the Green Flag.[9]

In the crisis of 1848 Joseph Brenan headed for the West. He travelled under the assumed name McCarthy, but was arrested at Gort, Co. Galway, on information received. It is not known whether the description in the

William Smith O'Brien.

Michael Doheny.

T. B. MacManus.

Patrick O'Donohoe.

T. Devin Reilly.

Richard O'Gorman, Junior.

John Savage.

YOUNG IRELAND LEADERS IN 1848

official *Hue and Cry* of him having a Cork accent sealed his fate![10] He was brought back to Dublin and committed to Newgate prison on a charge of high treason. On 18 August, with thirteen others, he was removed by war steamer to Belfast where they were met by a full military escort and a quay full of spectators only to be driven off at high speed to the new model prison at Crumlin Road. While they received special concessions one of Brenan's companions was very critical about the treatment of ordinary prisoners. He claimed, 'the man who designed Belfast Penitentiary, must like Dante have seen hell'.[11]

In December Brenan with some of his fellow prisoners was transferred to Kilmainham.[12] Although the authorities were confident enough to begin releases Brenan was still considered a high security risk. While some of the prisoners were highly critical of their conditions Brenan's only intervention outside the walls was one of literary compassion. When he heard that James Clarence Mangan was in very poor circumstances he organised a collection among the state prisoners as they 'were ashamed to see the tragedy of Robert Burns re-enacted in their country'.[13]

Dublin Castle decided to crack down on what they considered seditious articles and letters and ordered the sheriff and policemen to remove the prisoners to a secure part of the gaol. This attempt to enforce harsher conditions backfired and their cases was raised by Feargus O'Connor, the Chartist leader, in the House of Commons. Finally the Lord Lieutenant sanctioned the release of Brenan and five others on 1 March 1849.[14]

Although Brenan's spirit and belief in revolution was unbroken he had suffered personal tragedy. His girlfriend, Mary Ellen Downing, the precocious young girl who had contributed many poems to the *Nation* newspaper; who by her writings had stolen the heart of John O'Leary and many more, had suffered a severe nervous breakdown brought on by the total collapse of the Young Ireland movement and the jailing of its leaders.[15]

Brenan was appointed editor of the *Irishman* newspaper by Bernard Fulham. Fulham was an associate of Charles Gavan Duffy and had used the *Nation* printing press to launch the venture. Duffy never forgave him for this. One of Brenan's first tasks was to write an obituary for James Clarence Mangan.[16] Brenan was present with a few others, in a field at Rathmines, when the '49 movement was formally established. They would try to rebuild the Confederation as a secret oath-bound society for another attempt.

Meanwhile, Philip Gray left the South of Ireland and went to Paris to confer with John O'Mahony. For a short period he scraped an existence by teaching drawing, but soon returned home.[17] O'Mahony felt it would take years to build a convincing Irish revolutionary movement and that, in conscience, he could not use his influence to urge others to join the '49 movement when he was not willing to risk his own life.[18] However, O'Mahony's scruples had no effect on the Young Irelanders' enthusiasm for immediate war.

By May 1849 the movement was well established even though tensions had begun to appear within the leadership. James Fintan Lalor, whose belief that the land of Ireland belonged to the people of Ireland came closest to the old gospel of the Whiteboys, distrusted what he considered Joseph Brenan's impetuousity and rashness. That summer Lalor left Dublin on a recruitment drive and was accompanied by Thomas Clarke Luby. Luby from Dolphin's Barn, the son of a Protestant clergyman and nephew to a Trinity mathematics don had taken part on 27 July 1848 in a failed attempt by members of the Dublin Confederate Clubs to take Navan by way of Blanchardstown. When only a handful made the agreed rendezvous the attack was called off. Although Luby escaped undetected, among six captured were John Gray, Philip's brother, who was a butcher near Moore St. and one Richard Davis, a cabman, who paid dearly for his revolutionary fare – he was caught transporting rebels. Luby headed south but although at Kilmanagh, Co. Kilkenny, on 31 July 1848 he played no part in events other than to avoid arrest.[19]

By the end of May 1849 County Waterford was abuzz with rumours. The Authorities asked the Catholic clergy to speak against the new movement – and they were more than willing to do so. Yet, the Government was worried that the clergy had little success. Indeed, Dr. Robert Cane, for some the putative head of a revolutionary government in 1848, wrote to the *Kilkenny Journal* warning against the secret society which was making progress in 'his city and county'.[20]

In the same month the movement suffered its first setback when it had to call off an attempt to rescue William Smith O'Brien and the other leaders from Dublin's Richmond Bridewell. It was Edward O'Donohoe, Pat's brother, who made the request but the plan was abandoned following a letter sent out by John Martin to James Fintan Lalor.[21] John O'Leary had already failed when, in November 1848, his attempt to free Smith O'Brien and the others from Clonmel Gaol ended in his arrest and that of the rescue party at the Wilderness to the west of the town.

On 19 May an Irish gunman fired on the Queen's carriage from Green Park as it travelled down Constitution Hill towards Buckingham Palace. Victoria and her children were unhurt, as it appears that William Hamilton had only charged his pistol with gunpowder. While a Confederate or Chartist connection was mooted, the Home Office felt secure enough for the police to accept Hamilton's motive as being pure despair caused by unemployment. He had not worked at his trade as a bricklayer for some months. Poor Hamilton was said to be a native of Limerick but the Limerick newspapers claimed he was a Cork Protestant Orphan whereupon the Cork Protestant Orphans Society disclaimed all knowledge of him. He pleaded guilty at his trial in the Old Bailey and was sentenced to transportation for seven years and ended up in Van Diemen's Land.[22]

In late June and early July 1849 John Martin, Kevin Izod O'Doherty, William Smith O'Brien, Thomas Francis Meagher, Patrick O'Donohoe and Terence Bellew MacManus, the leaders of 1848, left Ireland, at her Majesty's pleasure, on board the *Mount Stuart Elphinstone* and the *Swift* and bound for Van Diemen's Land. They were completely unaware that another effort at revolution was underway.
With their enforced departure the way was now open for a royal visit. In early August Victoria with her husband Albert arrived in Cork. She came

to open her colleges, which were due to admit their first students in November. The City and Cove gave her a great welcome since quite apart from the Royal Navy both were booming because of the rush for Amerikay. Henceforth, Cove would be called Queenstown in her honour. The flattery continued when she departed for Dublin.

However, outside of the circle of wealthy ship-owners, merchants, public servants and those who were genuinely loyal to the Union, reaction was more muted. Indeed, it has been claimed that Joseph Brenan and his group seriously considered a plan to seize the young Queen if not to mount a day of action in Dublin. Dublin Castle was in no doubt that Brenan was a threat, for on 24 July an Inspector and seven policemen called to his home with a search warrant and read and removed his private correspondence. Be that as it may, the real effect of the visit appears to have been to spur them on to greater efforts and to ensure that there would be no turning back.

Brenan, still only 21, outlined his political views in the pamphlet *The Only Road or Hints for the Reorganisation of a National Party in Ireland.* These had already been printed in *The Irishman.* He was particularly scathing of the old Confederation:

> In reality it was the Repeal Association with a new coat on it. It was D'Olier Street, not Burgh Quay ... It mistook the cheers of Dublin for the applause of Ireland, and was more a reunion of *literati* than an assembly of revolutionists ... It sought for the constitution of '82, which was the triumph of landlordism and became the champion of aristocracy. It opened its arms for the land proprietors of Ireland, and in endeavouring to make patriots of tyrants, it wasted much talent and time ... The Confederation perished when John Mitchel was expelled.[24]

Brenan credited Mitchel with drawing his attention to the land question:

> It proved to us that a social revolution should precede a political one – that we should destroy landlordism before we could overthrow imperialism. The former supported the latter, and therefore, we should remove the one before we could rid the country of the other.[25]

Brenan argued that tenant right and the tenant leagues should form the basis of the new organisation and that in order to begin a favourable press and preliminary meetings were required. The "new clubs" 'would have all the merits of the clubs of '48, without any of their ludicrous boasting and threats'.[26]

Brenan was very clear on the strategy to be pursued:
> We must separate ourselves at once and forever from all English parties and factions. To our Irish and democratic brethren in Great Britain alone we must address ourselves. The English and Scotch Democrats are a rising, and will be a powerful body. In our day of struggle we may accept their aid, and in return we may aid them. In principle our cause is the same – the cause of self-government. With the same view, and to the same end, we must henceforth renounce and utterly despise the cant of conciliation ... We must no longer waste our strength and blast our hopes by seeking nominal converts in the ranks of the aristocracy. The national enemies of the people never join them save when they have some sinister or corrupt purpose to serve. Treachery and deceit have always followed from such alliances ... Above all, we must, to achieve Irish nationality rely solely and entirely upon the Democracy of Ireland. We must instruct, enlighten, elevate and strengthen our Democracy. [Meanwhile, he argued speed was essential.] There is not an hour to be lost. Each day sees the Irish Race nearer to annihilation.[27]

Finally Brenan exhorted the tenants of Ireland to use the harvest then growing in the fields, to feed themselves. He argued that anyone who gave up the harvest 'in a country richer than Canaan' was not deserving of sympathy.
> I say deliberately – and I feel that I say justly – may they be spurned from the doors of the nation – may they be cast forth from the family of man, and consigned to the famine graves which their own cowardice has digged.[28]

It must be presumed that Brenan's mooted national party would complement the secret revolutionary movement and support and greatly strengthen the latter. In practice all energies were concentrated on the secret movement. *The Only Road* first appeared as an editorial in the *Irishman* of 8 September as the Young Irelanders prepared the final details of their insurrection.[29]

On 5 September 1849 Brenan, Lalor, Gray, Luby and the others met at Clonmel and decided on Sunday 16 September as the date for the rising. There would be a simultaneous outbreak in Cork, Clare, Limerick, Kilkenny, Cashel, North Tipperary, Cappoquin and Dungarvan with forces based around Carrick-on-Suir being kept as a reserve. A committee of five would co-ordinate operations. However, of the five only Brenan, Lalor, Gray and Luby were willing to act.

Soon South Tipperary and Waterford were in a state of high excitement. On Sunday 9 September General McDonald left Clonmel with his forces and marched out to Ballingarry where he drew them up in full battle order. No one could be in any doubt as to the message he was delivering. Yet the conspirators were not intimidated. The four met, again at Clonmel, on Tuesday 11 September. Brenan would go to Cappoquin, Gray to Dungarvan, Lalor to Cashel and Luby to Kilkenny.[30] The die was now cast.

Their strategy was quite simple and drew on the movements perceived strengths and military, navy and police deployments. The main theatre of operations had been shifted westwards from 1848 to Southwest Tipperary and West Waterford. However, not too far west so as to bring them in direct contact with the Great Southern Railroad which, in the space of a year, had reached Limerick Junction, Mallow and was about to add Cork City to the network.[31] In both outbreaks in 1848 rail transport had made possible the so-called "flying columns" – rapid deployment of the military from the Curragh and police from the Phoenix Park.[32] Also, the threat posed by gunboats operating on the tidal stretches of the Suir and Blackwater had diminished with the withdrawal of the naval force stationed at Waterford in February 1849.[33] Similarly, the reduction in military strength at Dungarvan and the withdrawal of the garrison from Lismore Castle made for a favourable balance in West Waterford.[34] This area had seen quite a bit of unrest in 1848, for on the day Smith O'Brien and his forces battled the police at the Widow McCormack's, Richard Fitzpatrick was arrested for pinning a notice outside Cappoquin Church which called for 'Repeal or the Pike'. He had drawn a big pike to ensure the message got through to the greatest audience.[35] Similarly, in the same

JOSEPH BRENAN

town, when a military force attempted to move through on its way to the Comeragh mountains to mop up the followers of the Second Rising, in September 1848, they were severely obstructed by people warming themselves around a bonfire in the Main Street. The crowd greeted the Army with stones who in return charged with fixed bayonets. There were injuries on both sides and it required the intervention of a police support unit to clear the streets.

Cappoquin also had a long established Confederate Club which had been formed about March 1847 by John Williams of Dublin who was an influential member of the ruling Council of the Confederation. It was also the site of a major civil engineering project the Victoria Bridge, which began construction in September 1847. Employment here saved the lifes of many in the surrounding district but the bridge was not finished until 1851 and it is unclear how secure the workers' future seemed in 1849 given that the main contractor ran out of funds and died during construction. Finally, local intelligence had suggested that the door of Cappoquin barracks was generally kept open and only barred late at night so a genuine opportunity existed for a surprise attack.[36] Thus it can be seen that the conspirators had reasons for believing they had some prospects of success.

On Friday 14 September 1849 the *Cork Examiner* in an editorial entitled 'What does it mean?' tried to make sense of recent developments in the south of Ireland. The editor John Francis Maguire was very sympathetic to the Young Irelanders and had run extracts in the newspaper of what was to become Michael Doheny's *Felon's Track*. However, he was very much against any other attempts at revolution:

> We cannot credit, we do not believe that any insurrectionary movement is contemplated. Such a piece of insanity would be utterly incredible. Nothing but the destruction of individuals and the further prostration of the country could possibly follow.

His appeal had no effect on the conspirators rather by casting doubts on an impending rebellion, he helped to create more uncertainty and restored the element of surprise.

In the afternoon and evening of Sunday 16 September the men in Cappoquin and the surrounding districts prepared for action. Paddy Larry Walsh of Clonocogaile, the son of the largest farmer in the parish, gathered the men of Touraneena at the chapel and set off for Cappoquin. The column, which moved down from Melleray, included Seán Ó Caoimh of Glenafalla and Micheál Ó Haillí, Micil na bPort, from South Tipperary. Similarly, the men of Tourin and Camphire gathered at Owen Sullivan's cross.[37] Another group, that may have even included Joseph Brenan called to the Abbey, and were given milk and bread. They sought the blessing of the Prior – the Abbot was in America setting up a new monastery – but the Prior refused. They then asked for a loan of the monks' gun but naturally it was not given.[38]

By half past nine Brenan had enough men in position in the town to give the order, even though heavy rain meant a good deal of rebels were still moving up. So, in the gloom of an autumn evening he led out the attack. The rebels had donned white sashes and white belts to identify themselves so with their pikes and a scattering of firearms they approached the police barracks.

The constabulary force stationed in Cappoquin was housed in the old Army barracks – now Walsh's Hotel. There were ten men and a sub-inspector. At nine-o-clock that evening, a knock came to the door and the police were warned of the impending assault. There were only eight men in the station at the time, two being out on patrol in the town. They immediately bolted the door and loaded their rifles and one man ran to warn the sub-inspector and their comrades out in the town.[39]

While he got to the sub-inspector's house he was unable to contact the other two. One of them was lucky in that when he saw the approaching "army" he diplomatically retired into a local hotel. However, sub-constable James Owens was made of sterner stuff but ended up with serious pike wounds. Although the rebels had lost the element of surprise they used their pikes to break the windows of the barracks but were frustrated by the bars. Without artillery it is very difficult to take a fortified building. Despite the firing of the police they brought up a cart

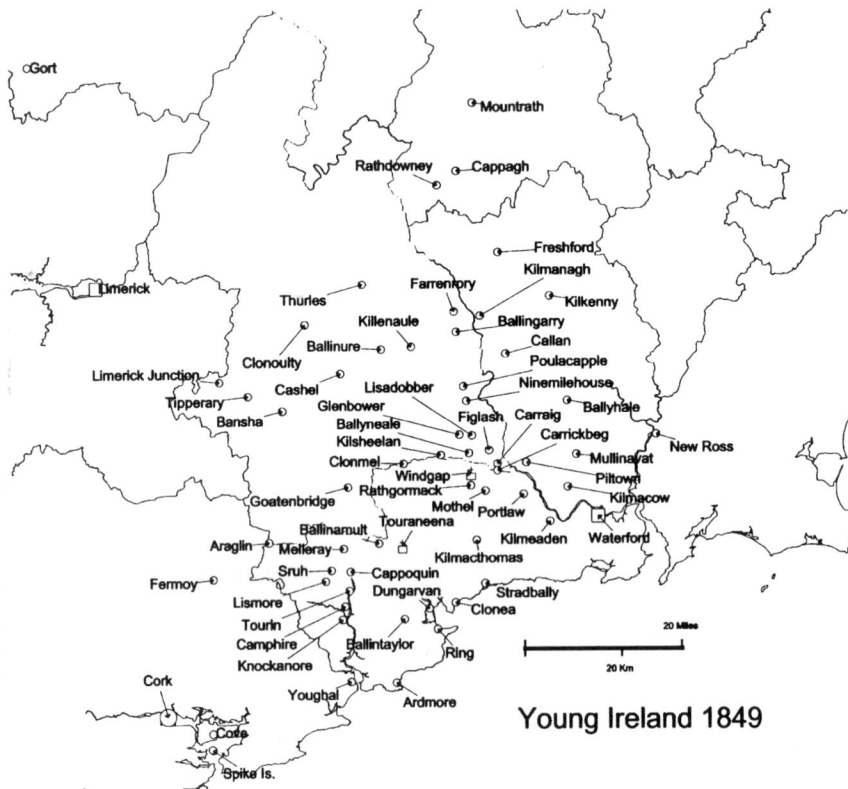

Young Ireland 1849

YOUNG IRELAND, 1849

and attempted to gain entry through the upper story of the barracks. The result was still in doubt until the rebels came under fire from Sir Richard Keane's gate. Séamas Ó Caoimh (grandnephew of the man who fought at Cappoquin) in his autobiography *An Sléibhteánach* describes the dilemma the rebels found themselves in: *'Bhí na hÉireannaigh idir dhá tine lae Bealtaine'* (They were caught between two bonefires on May day).[40] Young James Donohoe, of the town, was mortally wounded, shot through the heart. The Rebels broke and ran. The intervention of John Yorick, Keane's mountain ranger, decided the night.

On the Monday the local magistrates rushed to the town. Henry Villiers Stuart, Lord Stuart de Decies, the hero of the Catholic Emancipation county election of 1826, swore in special constables to defend the town. However, they were soon relieved as the 7th or Royal Fusiliers arrived from Youghal. Thus began the military occupation of Cappoquin, which would continue to September 1852. Troops were also sent from Clonmel, to occupy Ballinamult barracks, in an attempt to secure and subdue the district of Sliabh gCua.[41]

It soon became obvious that while Cappoquin had led neither Dungarvan, Cashel or Kilkenny had followed. The men of Dungarvan were to gather at Ballinamuck, just outside the town, but it must be presumed they either got cold feet or else it was decided at the last moment to concentrate all forces at Cappoquin.[42] It is difficult to know what weight should be given to the alleged discovery by the authorities of the suborning of members of the garrison in Dungarvan Castle particularly as it appears no soldiers were ever put on trial for what would be a capital offence.[43]

John O'Leary, who later became famous, as a Fenian was due to lead a contingent from Tipperary Town to liase with James Fintan Lalor at Cashel but when only about 50 turned up at the meeting place he dismissed them and set off alone. O'Leary met Lalor and they proceeded to Clonoulty where they gathered some support but they still called off the operation. A modern biographer of Lalor has wondered about Lalor and O'Leary's courage.[44] As for Luby he never got to Kilkenny but spent some days in Cashel bridewell having been arrested by the Ballinure police as being a suspicious character. He was in the house of Thomas Mara, a farmer, with a Mr. Ryan from Clonmel and James Garvan, a shoemaker, when they were taken and they had military manuals in their possession.[45] Thus even had Brenan been successful at Cappoquin and led his forces to Clonmel – which appears to have been the plan – it is unlikely they could have overcome the regular army unless they hoped to catch them in their beds. Moreover, it would take extreme discipline to hold his tiny forces when they would reach Irishtown and the Old Bridge and discover that the army of Cappoquin stood alone.

However, this is mere speculation. Brenan and most of the leaders at Cappoquin managed to escape. Brenan left Cork in October for America, never to return. It appears he had hidden out in the Waterford Mountains until the time came to don his disguise and take a coal boat to Wales. In the same month his girlfriend, Ellen Mary Downing, entered the North Presentation Convent as a novice. She had recovered from her illness but had broken with revolution for the religious life. In America, Brenan resumed his journalistic career and later married Mary Savage, whose brother John had led the attack at Portlaw during the Second Rising of 1848. Brenan renewed his ties with John Mitchel when the latter escaped from Van Diemen's Land. He eventually settled in New Orleans but suffered greatly from ill health. Like Mitchel he espoused the cause of States Rights which at the time meant you supported slavery in those States in which it was legal. He still kept up in his interest in poetry and wrote *Ballads of the Young South.* He had just started to publish a new newspaper, the *New Orlean Times,* when he died in 1857. He is buried in the Old French Cemetery. He was honoured with a full obituary in the *Cork Examiner* and it was probably John Francis Maguire who wrote, 'The dust which covers his remains will be upon one of Ireland's most gifted, brave and loyal gentlemen'.[46]

As for Mary Ellen Downing the religious life proved unsuitable for she was dogged by ill health. She recovered, to succeed her mother as matron of the Cork Fever Hospital in 1860, but an internal dispute forced her resignation. Her old admirer, John O'Leary, published her religious poems in the *Irish People*, proving that Catholicism and Fenianism were not incompatible, but she broke with the paper when she heard that it had criticised some priest. She died in 1869, at the age of 41. Some time after her death her collected religious poems were published.[47]

Paddy Larry Walsh went on the run and after many escapades he arrived at the Quay in Dungarvan only to find the town full of policemen. Undaunted, Paddy Larry put on an old Irish cloak and headed for the boat. He had to pass two policemen and everything seemed all right until one of the policemen turned and walked back toward him – but it was only to mutter under his breath – *Go néirí an t-ádh leat a Phádraig* (Good luck to you Paddy). Paddy Larry safely arrived in the United States. He returned home in 1865, when his brother died, to inherit the farm. He never made a great fist of farming, but continued to keep up his ties with the various Irish revolutionary movements. He died in 1915, at the age of 93.[48]

Micheál Caomhánach (Michael Cavanagh), the best known revolutionary of the period from Cappoquin and his friend Hugh Collender though fiercely hunted by the authorities, got away to America. Caomhánach achieved literary success in Irish and English and became an influential Fenian, serving as secretary to John O'Mahony. His important biography of Thomas Francis Meagher was published in 1892. It was to have been followed by a biography of John O'Mahony and a full account of events in 1848 and 1849, but it is unclear whether Caomhánach managed to complete this work. He died in 1900, but not before he had helped to establish a Chair in Celtic Studies in the Catholic University of Washington. Incidentally, the first holder of the chair was Fr. Richard Henebry of Mount Bolton, Portlaw, who later helped to set up Ring College, which proved to be one of the most influential institutions in the Irish language revival. Dan Magrath, Caomhánach's cousin, a saddler, who also played a significant part in events at Cappoquin likewise managed to reach America. A Fenian, successful businessman and friend of John O'Mahony, he died in 1888 and is buried in the Catholic cemetery of Marshall, Missouri. Another saddler to end up out West was Magrath and Cavanagh's friend, Bob Ward from Ballyhale. He earlier spent some years in Baltimore, Maryland. America did little to modify Ward's extreme nationalism. From *An Sléibtheánach,* we know that both Séan Ó Caoimh of Glenafalla and Micil an bPort ended up Stateside. Séan Ó Caoimh eventually settled in Cincinnatti, Ohio.[49]

Finally, Hugh Collender achieved great wealth in the United States and made his fortune in billiard tables. In 1873 he built a factory at Stamford Connecticut and began to develop that part of the nearby town of Darien, which became known as Collender's Point. In 1879 he merged his company with his main rival in Cincinnatti and in 1884 this became known as the Brunswick Balke Collender Company. Hugh was President from 1886 until his death in 1890 at the age of 61. The company still exists as the Brunswick Corporation and is a major leisure mulitinational.[49]

HUGH COLLENDER

However, not all from Cappoquin were so lucky and it is chiefly their fate and the fate of the rest of the Young Ireland prisoners that will concern

- 24 -

us.

It was John Yorick, Sir Richard Keane's mountain ranger, the man who turned the rebels' flank who denounced John Donohoe and Luke Lennon to the authorities. They, together with two others, were taken away from Cappoquin on the afternoon of Wednesday 19 September 1849. The whole town turned out to cheer them and demand their release. One account states that Howley the R.M. twice read the Riot Act and threatened to order the military and police to fire on the prisoners unless they were left proceed to Dungarvan.[50]

The inquests on James Donohoe and sub-constable James Owens were held on Thursday 20 September. Fr. Seán Walsh C.C was asked for his opinion as to what had happened. He had no doubts that it was purely a local incident directed by the lower classes in the town whose only aim was plunder. He described them as, 'as fine a set of ruffians as could be found in any town in Ireland'.[51] Events would soon cause him to reflect on these words as Nicholas Foran, Bishop of Waterford & Lismore, took drastic action. On 30 September he accepted the resignation of Fr. John Breathnach, the elderly parish priest and the other curate Fr. Patrick Wall. Fr. Walsh did not escape either and was quickly re-assigned to the rural parish of Knockanore and Kilwatermoy.[52]

The arrests continued. John Brien, a wool spinner from Cork, who arrived in the town about ten months before the rising, gave valuable information to the authorities. These efforts were stepped up following another incident at Cappoquin on Wednesday 26 September. A Royal Fusilier sentry claimed to have been attacked by three men with pikes as he stood guard under the arch of the market house.[53] On 1 October several houses in Dungarvan were raided by the police, including that of John D. Hearn in Church St. Patrick Howley R.M. believed that there had been an actual muster of rebels at Ballinamuck on 16 September, led by Hearn. He described him as 'a very well educated young man but of broken down fortune ... son to a late sub-sheriff of the county'.[54] The police also raided his brother's house in Waterford City and found unlicenced guns and gunpowder. On the following day Howley reported to Sir Thomas

COLLENDER'S BILLIARD FACTORY

Redington, the Under Secretary, that his informant had come up with a name for the Cappoquin attack, 'Brenan of *The Irishman*'.[55] The authorities also arrested John Kennedy of Cove Hill, Clonea for having unlicensed firearms and Gerry Morrissey, a Dungarvan publican with 'numerous connections among the farming class'.[56] Morrissey just happened to be the employer of one Paddy Larry Walsh so it did not help when ammunition was found in his house. He was released on bail, but his drink licence and that of two other Dungarvan publicans, Tobin and Browne, was withdrawn. So many people were on the run that it was remarked, 'the county will soon be pretty thinned of young men'.[57] One of the final arrests was at Mount Odell – the man John Walsh of Tourin - the nephew of Fr. Spratt the new parish priest of Cappoquin and brother of Fr. Richard Walsh the new curate. He had been seen at Owen Sullivan's cross with his gun and in company with his three workmen who were also arrested.

The prisoners were tried at the County Spring and Summer Assizes for 1850. In the March Assizes James Crotty and John Donohoe, from Cappoquin, Mathew Joy from Carrickbeg and Luke and John Lennon from Cappoquin were convicted and sentenced to transportation for fourteen years. The Crown was unable to sustain a prosecution against Cornelius Daly, the Cappoquin tailor, who had been charged with the murder of sub-constable Owens or to even substitute a lesser charge and he was freed from custody in May.[58] In the July Assizes Patrick Cashman, James Bourke and Thomas Hely were acquitted of having arms and pikes on the night of the attack. Similarly, Catherine Power, a labourer from Ring who had been arrested with Bridget Fahey was found not guilty of being armed and attacking the police barracks. The carpenter, Maurice Flahavan, who had four pikes in his Cappoquin workshop when arrested, had absconded while on bail and did not appear when his name was called. John Hearn was given one week in prison. However, James Casey from Clonmel, James Lyons, James Ryan, Thomas Ryan and Thomas Wall all from Cappoquin got fourteen years with John Walsh and his three workmen Edward Tobin from Araglin, Thomas Donovan from Sruh and Richard Brien from Tourin all getting seven years.[59] Of the fourteen sentenced only eleven were transported. The Ryan brothers pleaded guilty and had their sentences commuted to two years imprisonment.[60] John Lennon, Luke's brother, died in Spike Island Prison in 1852.

The Donohoes of Cappoquin paid heavily for the Rising. James at only 21 years was dead. His first cousin, John, was in Spike Island waiting to be sent over the ocean for fourteen years. John's sister Mary Griffin who had married well in Baltimore, Maryland rushed home. She would bring her brother away to the United States if only the Government would agree. But her efforts came to nothing.[61] John's parents Michael and Margaret sent a memorial or petition to Clarendon, the Lord Lieutenant, in which they gave their version of the events of that fateful Sunday night. John Donohoe had been out in Dromroe – about two miles east of the town – meeting his fiancée Bridget Browne. He saw Bridget home- apparently she lived seven miles from Cappoquin – and then got a lift back to town on a car. As the car approached the town they met people running in the opposite direction. The Donohoes also questioned John Yorick's crucial identification of their son given that the night was dark. Dublin Castle sought the comments of sub-inspector Slattery of Cappoquin. He described John's character 'as being notoriously bad so far as being a drunken, riotous and disorderly person'.[62] He also described many of the people who signed the memorial as being disaffected. The authorities would not budge!

On 13 September 1850 seven of the Cappoquin rebels left Queenstown, on board the *Hyderabad*, for Van Diemen's Land, leaving only John Donohoe, the Lennons, Mathew Joy and James Crotty in Spike. In April 1851 Luke had to say goodbye to his brother John as he and the other three were moved to Dublin to await their convict transport. John, a labourer had scrofula, a type of tuberculosis, was unfit to travel and died in the prison hospital on 30 January 1852 aged 26.[63] Michael Donohoe made one last effort to save his son. He explained to the Government that John's mother Margaret, who had been buried that February, had died of a broken heart as a result of being deprived of her only son. He also dwelt on his own service as a soldier in the Napoleonic wars but it was all to no avail. The government's final decision was 'law to take its course'.[64]

Notes:

1. *Waterford Chronicle,* 16 September 1848.
2. J. Savage, '98 and '48 *The Modern Revolutionary History and Literature of Ireland,* New York, 1860, p. 353; J. O'Mahony, 'The Young Ireland Rising', in J. Maher ed., *Chief of the Comeraghs,* Mullinahone 1957, p.73.
3. T.C. Luby, *Irish News,* March 14 1857.
4. Newgate Prison Register 1848, N.A., Prisons 1/12/2, no. 1509; *Cork Examiner,* 5 March 1849.
5. A hoe.
6. See p. iv.
7. M. Cavanagh, 'Joseph Brenan', *Young Ireland,* 27 June 1885.

8. Cavanagh, *Memoirs of Gen. Thomas Francis Meagher*, Worcester Mass. 1892, p. 243.

9. J Devoy, *Recollections of an Irish Rebel*, New York 1929, p. 267; M. Doheny, *The Felon's Track*, Dublin, 1951; O'Mahony, op. cit., pp. 70-1. The faction leader who so impressed Michael Doheny (pp. 201-2) was probably Power of Graigavalla, Rathgormack, head of the Gows. See also M.B. Kiely & W. Nolan, 'Politics, Land and Rural Conflict in County Waterford 1830-1845', in W. Nolan & T. Power eds., *Waterford History & Society*, Dublin 1992, p. 478.

10. *Cork Examiner*, 4, 9, 21 August 1848.

11. Ibid., 20 December 1848.

12. Kilmainham Prison Register 1848, N.A., Prisons 1/10/8, no. 2118.

13. *Cork Examiner*, 10 January 1849.

14. Ibid., January 8, 22, February 2, 26, 28; 5 March 1849.

15. Sr. M.A. Downing, *Voices from the Heart Sacred Poems*, new & rev. ed., Dublin 1881, pp. xii-xvi; L.M. O'Toole, 'The Women Writers of the Nation', in M.J. MacManus ed., *Thomas Davis and Young Ireland*, Dublin 1945, p.120.

16. *The Irishman*, 23 June 1849.

17. Luby, *Irish News*, op. cit. Feach freisin ar T Ó Néill, *Fiontán Ó Leathlobhair*, Baile Átha Cliath 1962, lch. 99.

18. B Ó Cathaoir, 'John O'Mahony 1815-1877', in *Capuchin Annual* 1977, p. 182.

19. Luby, N.L.I., MS 332; Luby, *Irish News*, op. cit; Kilmainham Prison Register 1848, op. cit., nos. 994, 998.

20. *Waterford Mail* 2 June 1849; P.C. Howley to T. Redington, 8 May 1849, N.A., O.P., 29/138/1849.

21. Luby, *Irish Nation*, 28 January 1882.

22. *Waterford Mail*, 23, 26, 30 May, 2, 20 June 1849; *Cork Examiner* 23, 30 May 1849

23. *Tipperary Free Press*, 28 July 1849.

24. J. Brenan, *The Only Road*, Dublin 1849.

25. Ibid.

26. Ibid.

27. Ibid.

28. Ibid.

29. *The Only Road* was published on 22 September 1849. See add. in *The Irishman* of same date.

30. T.P. O'Neill, 'Fintan Lalor and the 1849 Movement', in *An Cosantóir*, vol X, no. 4, April 1950, pp. 173-79.

31. K.A. Murray & D.B. McNeill, *The Great Southern and Western Railway*, Dublin 1976, p. 18.

32. *Waterford Mail*, 16 September 1848.

33. *Waterford News*, 2 February 1849.

34. Ibid., 19 January 1849; *Cork Examiner*, 28 March 1849.

35. Waterford County Gaol Register 1848, N.A., Prisons 1/39/2, no. 833.

36. *Waterford Mail*, 23 September 1848, 13, 20 & 24 July 1850 & 5 March 1851; Cavanagh, Meagher, p. 112.

37. Ibid., 10 October 1849, 17 July 1850; Howley to Redington, 1 October 1849, N.A., O.P., 29/411/1849; F.X. O'Leary, 'The Black Christmas A Fragment of West Waterford History', in *Cork Holly Bough*, 1956, pp.17-33; S. Ó Caoimh, *An Sléibhteánach*, Magh Nuad 1989, lch. 15.

38. *Cork Examiner*, 21 September 1849; *Waterford Mail*, 26 September 1849.

39. *Waterford Mail*, 29 September 1849; P. Slattery to Howley, 17 September 1849, N.A., O.P., 29/370/1849.

40. Ó Caoimh, op. cit., lch. 16.

41. Howley to Redington, 17 September 1849, N.A., ibid; H. Stuart de Decies to Redington, 27 November 1850, N.A., O.P., 29/263/1850; O.P., 29/177 & 29/221/1852.

42. Howley to Redington, 1 October 1850, op. cit.

43. A.M. Breen, *The Cappoquin Rebellion 1849*, Thurston, Suffolk 1998, pp. 41-2. In his unpublished memoirs James Francis Xavier O'Brien, who was prominent in Dungarvan Confederate circles claims he received no notice of the rising until after it took place. He presumed it was because of his youth. However, this rings a little hollow as he was then 21 years of age. It is certainly true that he had to flee from the authorities. See P. McCarthy,'Francis Xavier O' Brien (1828-1905): Dungarvan-born Fenian' in *Decies*, no. 54, 1998, pp. 107, 112, 114.

44. J. O'Leary, *Recollections of Fenians & Fenianism*, London 1896, vol 1, p. 39; D.N. Buckley, *James Fintan Lalor:* Radical, Cork 1990, p. 24.

45. Luby, MS 332, op. cit., pp. 14-5; *Cork Examiner*, 21, 28 September 1849.

46. *Cork Examiner*, 17 June 1857. See also *Daily Picayune*, 28, 29, May 1857; Cavanagh, *Young Ireland*, 18 July 1885; D.J. O'D., 'Joseph Brenan', in *Irish Book Lover*, vol v, June 1914, pp. 189-91; *Louisiana Newspapers 1794-1940*, Louisiana State University 1940, p. 123.

47. J.F. Conlon, 'Mary of the Nation', *Evening Echo*, 21 January 1966 and *Some Irish Poets & Musicians*, Midleton 1974, p.31; D. Ó Mathúna, 'Banfhile ó Chorcaigh Mary an Nation', *Agus*, Deireadh Fomhár 1990, Iml. xxx, lcha. 20-2; Will of Julia Downing, *Wills Ireland* 1860; *Cork Examiner*, 28 May, 20 June 1860, 28 January 1869.

48. O'Leary, op. cit., D. Ó Cadla, Cáthair na Leige, Béaloideas.
49. D. Breathnach & M. Ní Mhurchú, *1882-1982 Beathaisnéis A hAon*, Baile Átha Cliath 1986, lcha. 19-20, *1882-1992 Beathaisnéis A Dó*, Baile Átha Cliath 1990, lcha. 35-6; Cavanagh, Meagher, op. cit., pp. 112, 148, 263, 283-4; P.E. Mac Fhinn, *An tAthair Micheál P. Ó hIceadha*, Baile Átha Cliath 1974, lch. 22; Ó Caoimh, op. cit., lch. 16; R. Kogan, *Brunswick The Story of an American Company The First 150 Years*, Lake Forest, Illinois 1995, pp 15-20; H.J., Case & S.W., Cooper, *Town of Darien 1641-1935*, Darien, Conn., 1935, pp. 10-12.
50. *Waterford Mail*, 22 September 1849; J. Yorick Memorial, 2 September 1850, N.A., O.P., 29/206/1850; Howley to Redington, 18 September 1849, ibid., 29/380/1849.
51. *Cork Examiner*, 21 September 1849. In order to distinguish between Fr. John Walsh parish priest and curate an Irish English version of their names has been used in the text. The quote is believed to have come from the curate.
52. See St. Mary's Cappoquin Marriage Register, October 1849, Knockanore Baptismal Register 1848-50 and *Battersby's Catholic Directory* 1848-52.
53. *Waterford Mail*, 3 October 1849; Breen, op. cit, p. 82. 12 Midnight? – sentry fires shot, rifle loaded but no bullet? – hempen belt saves him from possible fatal pike thrust?
54. Howley to Redington, 1 October 1849, op. cit.
55. Ibid., 2 October 1849, N.A., O.P., 29/415/1849.
56. *Waterford Mail*, 13 & 10 October 1849.
57. Ibid., 20 October 1849.
58. Waterford County Gaol Register 1849, N.A., Prisons 1/39/3, no. 1323; *Waterford Mail*, 6,13, March 1850.
59. *Waterford Mail*, July 17 1850; Waterford County Gaol 1849, op. cit., nos. 1337-8. Howley to Redington, 18 September 1849, op. cit.
60. Petition of T. & J. Ryan, N.A., C.R.F., R28/1850.
61. Petition of M. Griffin, 15 July 1850, Governor of Spike Island Prison, 3 August 1850, ibid., D41/1850.
62. Slattery, 19 July 1850, petitions of Mh. & Mg. Donohoe, 26 June, 30 July 1850, petition of Mh. Donohoe, 19 September 1850, ibid.
63. Spike Island Convict Register, N.L.I., MS 3016, no. 2727; Waterford County Gaol 1849, op. cit., no. 1329.
64. Petition of Mh. Donohoe 29 April 1851 and Note of 30 April 1850, N.A., C.R.F., D41/1850.

CHAPTER 2 BERMUDA

On 17 May 1851, John Donohoe and his three companions sailed from Kingstown, on board the ship *Bride* for Ireland Island. Also on board were Thomas Burke of Figlash and William Kelly of Ballyneale who had been transported for ten years for their part in the attack on Glenbower barracks in September 1848. The *Bride* took a westerly course and sailed over 3,000 miles out into the Atlantic and five weeks later reached the colony of Bermuda. The first week of the voyage was very stormy and the high seas sickened many of the convicts. The Governor of Bermuda was expecting English prisoners but the jails of Ireland were so full that the British government had to do something.[1]

Bermuda has been described as being like a shepherd's crook with the outside of the crook pointing towards the United States. It was made up of a series of islands which were either interconnected by causeway or ferry and in total was only 24 miles in length and varying from 300 yards to 1½ miles in breadth. Ireland Island was at the top of the crook and contained the great naval dockyard, which serviced the Royal Navy's Caribbean and North Atlantic fleets.

John and the others were soon put to work in the dockyard and housed in those dismasted and converted ships known as hulks. Awaiting them was another Waterford revolutionary William Doyle who had been transported for his part in the 1848 attack on Portlaw. Bermuda has a beautiful, almost tropical climate, which is extremely pleasant from January to June. In July and August it got very hot and there was always the danger of hurricanes. The climate was so benign that the soil produced three crops of Irish potatoes a year. The Island's only other drawback was that yellow jack or yellow fever appeared intermittently.

However, life in the hulks, even allowing for the fact the prisoners went ashore each day, was very injurious to health. The *Dromedary,* the *Coromandel* and the *Medway* were not actually afloat, but beached on what was called the camber at Ireland Island. They have been described as being 'grounded in thick muck, insufficiently ventilated, swarming with cockroaches and vermin and housing a crowd of ill-fed and depressed men'.[2]   The harrowing Report of William John Williams, Inspector of Prisons on the Irish hulks in the 1830s had allowed the innovative Under Secretary Thomas Drummond to end this form of penal confinement. However, the English hulks and those at Gibralter and Bermuda were not affected. Although the same Inspector produced an equally damning report into the general treatment and conditions of convicts in the hulk at Woolwich in 1847 it was not until 1857 that the English hulks were abolished, with Bermuda following in 1862.[3]

The days and years passed and John Donohoe and the other six Young Irelanders in their convict garb of straw hat, blouse with the name of their hulk and their number printed on it and rough trousers worked away. Time made them familiar with every inch of their small part of Bermuda:

> Ireland Island seems a strong fortress. A handsome range of buildings crowns the Hill in the middle of the island; this is a barrack, with government storehouses adjoining all having arched and bomb-proof roofs. In front of this the hill is deeply scarped, down to the level of the dockyard; and in rear the slope is cut into terraces mounted with cannon. The barrack hill communicates by a long, sweeping line of fortifications with another hill on the extreme north of the island, which is occupied with other government buildings and surrounded by powerful batteries. In the crescent formed by all these works, to the eastward, is the naval dockyard with stores, offices and wet dock. Some of these are vast and sumptuous buildings.[4]

In 1851 an English author had been inspired to publish his impressions of Bermuda from notes he had put together at the time of the failure of the Young Ireland rebellion. He saw Bermuda as a great deterrent and enthusiastically:

> Would advice those who are quiet in Ireland to remain so, as a visit to Ireland Island, Bermuda, at the Queen's expense, in a grey jacket, and small clothes, ribbed stockings, and a coal heaver's hat, the leg being decked with a bright steel anklet, with plenty of work, in a tropical climate, for three half pence a day, is very romantic when patriotically acquired. But depend upon it, even this so-called patriotism, will have cooled after ten years of such a life.[5]

Nearly half a century earlier Thomas Moore in a brief sojourn in Bermuda

as a civil servant wrote of his island idyll:

> Could you but see the scenery fair,
> That now beneath my window lies,
> You'd think that Nature lavished there
> Her purest waves, her softest skies,
> To make a heaven for love to sigh in
> For bards to live, and saints to die in.[6]

The boredom and routine of prison life was only punctuated by frequent illness with perhaps a visit to the *Tenedos* hospital ship, transfers from one hulk to another and the deaths of fellow prisoners.

The case of William Quinlan combined all the horrors of the Famine and Irish agrarian violence with bureaucratic wrangling and the inability of the penal system to deal with a prisoner who was officially deemed sane. Quinlan was convicted at County Tipperary Spring Assizes of 1849 for the murder of three keepers at Rossadrehid near Bansha in the Galtee foothills, in October 1848. The occupier of some lands nearby was in arrears with his Poor Law rates and the Collector had installed keepers (bailiffs) to secure payment. It was claimed at the trial that a group met out on the mountains and decided to go hunting hares and bailiffs. Early on a Sunday morning the group, which included Quinlan, pursued the keepers who managed to get refuge in a nearby house. However, the door was broken down and two of the unfortunate men were shot on their knees in the kitchen with another battered to death in the yard. Hugh Kennedy, son in law of the landholder in question, Redmond Brien, was acquitted at the trial but William Quinlan received a death sentence and was to be hanged on 9 April 1849.[7]

Quinlan's demeanour in the dock when he appeared to be in a private reverie and completely unaware of the seriousness of proceedings raised serious concerns about his mental state. While his sentence was later commuted to transportation for life the Inspectors of Lunatic Asylums in Ireland were convinced his derangement was simulated. When he arrived in Bermuda in December 1849, on the *Pestonjee Bomanjee* with William Doyle of Portlaw and 299 others, James Hall the medical superintendent on the *Tenedos* hospital ship was convinced he was dealing with a genuine lunatic. Even T.H. Keown the surgeon on the *Pestonjee Bomanjee* saw the diagnosis of feigning insanity 'as still a doubtful case'.[8] Hall's concern was heightened when Quinlan tried to commit suicide by cutting the veins in the bend of each elbow with a tin mug. Governor Elliot sought to have Quinlan removed 'to a madhouse in the United Kingdom'[9] but the advice from Whitehall was that he would have to go back to Ireland. However, Dublin Castle was still convinced of Quinlan's sanity. In July 1852 Elliot once more sought permission to return his insane prisoner who 'has become so ungovernable as to render his detention at his depot, where we have no proper means of taking care of mad prisoners, highly inexpedient'.[10]
However, the problem soon solved itself when William Quinlan died on board the hulk *Medway* on 19 September 1852. An inquest returned a

verdict of bowel constriction.

Only six of the seven Young Ireland prisoners survived the great yellow fever outbreak, which held Bermuda in thrall from August to December 1853. Almost a quarter of the island's garrison perished with the convicts losing about 10% of their number of approximately 1600 – amongst them poor William Doyle of Portlaw.[11] Doyle was with a group of 300 Young Irelanders, under John Savage and Philip Gray, who attacked Portlaw Police barracks at five-o-clock in the morning of Tuesday 12 September 1848. The building was defended by eight policemen and a local magistrate. The attack soon petered out and an attempt to burn the building failed. A young man called Wade, about 20 years of age, the son of a stocking vendor from Kerry was shot dead and two others wounded. There were no casualties on the police side. Doyle was arrested some time later at Ross, just outside Portlaw, and was described as being a comfortable farmer. He was transported for ten years for his part in the attack at the County Waterford Spring Assizes for 1849. In the prison records he was described as a labourer and left a wife and two children in Ireland. He was frequently ill while in Bermuda and would not have been in great shape to battle the yellow fever outbreak. He died on the *Tenedos* hospital ship at 10.00 a.m. on 3 October 1853 at the age of 32.[12] He was buried in the convict cemetery on tiny Watford Island. The Catholic chaplain Fr. Thomas Lyons died on 9 October. However, the epidemic eventually abated.

Although the coast of North Carolina was 600 miles to the west the Authorities always made sure that the American boats were carefully supervised. Had John Donohoe and his comrades been prominent leaders like John Mitchel – who had spent from 20 June 1848 to 22 April 1849 in Bermuda – the American Irish might have organised a rescue attempt.[13] However, John Donohoe was not forgotten in Cappoquin. In 1854 his father Michael wrote to the Governor of Bermuda asking for his son to be sent home now that he had served five years. Michael Donohoe reflected on the irony of life for in 1808 as a young man he had served in Bermuda. Moreover, in 1814 he was with the Royal Marines on Lake Champlain in Vermont as they fought against the United States.[14] Similarly, Bridget Joy

Batteries. The 'Medway.' The 'Coromandel.' The 'Dromedary.' Victualling Stores. Keep and Commissioner's House.

A View of Ireland Island, Bermuda, in June, 1848.

of Millvale, Carrrickbeg the widowed mother of Mathew Joy once more interceded on her son's behalf with the following petition:

> That memoralist humbly begs leave to approach your Excellency with feeling of deepest humiliation, and at the same time asking your Excellency's pardon on behalf of a poor widow's son now a prisoner in Irelands Island, and whose only crime since his birth is the simple one for which he was transported to your colony for the period of fourteen years.
>
> That memoralist under the melancholy circumstances which have deprived her in old days of the protection of a good son, now humbly begs your Excellency will take into your kind consideration the nature of the case for which he was sent from his family and his native home.
>
> That memoralist begs to say that Ireland being in a disturbed state at the time memoralist's son with others were found guilty for an attack on the Police barracks of Cappoquin in the County of Waterford ..., altho it was proved on his trial by two respectable witnesses that he had no hand in the affair.
>
> That memoralist humbly prays your Excellency now that the prisoner Mathew Joy is going on his fifth year in exile, will be graciously pleased to send him home to support a poor wife and two helpless children whose humble prayers and benedictions will be offered up on high for your Excellency's health and prosperity in unison with the memoralist whose only wish on earth is to see her beloved son once more returned to his maternal turf ...[15]

This plea for clemency was supported by a number of the Catholic and Established Church clergy around Carrick-on-Suir, some magistrates and a solicitor.

Both parents' requests were passed from the Colonial Office to the Home Office but John and Mathew were not sent home.[16] By now there were only five Young Irelanders left for William Kelly of Ballyneale, whose health had been poor for some time, died of dysentery on 9 May.

Kelly, a labourer, took part in the Second Rising of 1848 and was with a group of around 100, who at seven-o-clock in the evening of 12

September 1848 advanced on the police barracks at Glenbower. The barracks commanded the junction of the Carrick road with the main Clonmel to Kilkenny road. The police had been ordered to fall back on Carrick-on-Suir but unfortunately for the rebels were still in the barracks when they arrived. Although the rebels captured some of the police equipment and clothes, which the police had abandoned outside, the attack failed when young Patrick Keating of Rathclarish was shot dead and the Nine Mile House police, on retreat to Carrick, caught the Young Irelanders in the rear. Although William Kelly pleaded guilty at the Tipperary Spring Assizes of 1849 he was sentenced to ten years transportation for attacking the barracks. He was aged 30 when he died on the *Tenedos* hospital ship.[17]

The other Glenbower prisoner Thomas Burke was the first of the Young Irelanders to be sent home. He arrived in Queenstown on the barque *Markland* on 10 March 1855 having become eligible for release under licence.[18] There was the short formality of a stay in prison and then home to Figlash. Unlike, Kelly, Burke had protested his innocence at the Tipperary Spring Assizes of 1849 but was still convicted and sentenced to 10 years transportation. When he appealed from the dock to Judge Jackson, 'I have a helpless family, my Lord'. The reply was 'I am sorry to hear it, and let it be a warning to the poor people not to oppose the loyal force of the country when as a necessary consequence such opposition must inevitably be suppressed'.[19] Later, the Judge did confirm that it was a case in which the executive might exercise clemency. He had been asked to comment on a memorial from Burke to Clarendon, the Lord Lieutenant, in which he claimed to have been 'innocently persuaded to assemble with the rest of his distracted and betrayed countrymen'.[20] However, any hopes in this regard were shattered by the events of 1849. In his final petition to government from Mountjoy Gaol in March 1851 he described his wife and four children as being reduced to the 'most disastrous state of poverty and destitution'[21] but he was still sent to Bermuda.

Only Mathew Joy of the remaining four was well enough to fight a major fire, which broke out in the Dockyard on the evening of 13 June 1855. It was eventually controlled using bucket chains composed of the convicts but rumours abounded that they were about to rise. Despite the suspicions of sabotage the rewards offered by the authorities went unclaimed.[22]

Six years earlier, on 3 July 1849, Irish convicts on the hulk *Medway* paid dearly for an attempt to prevent the flogging of James Cronin of Limerick for insubordination. His elder brother Thomas appealed in Irish to his fellow prisoners who followed him in rushing the barrier, which separated the main deck from the quarter deck, where the flogging was to take place. The Convict Guard fired two volleys and the affair resulted in three deaths and twelve serious injuries. No assistance was rendered to any of the dying or wounded until James Cronin received his 24 lashes. While Governor Elliot upheld the conduct of the authorities the other casualty of the affair was the overseer Francis Burdet Black who was removed from his position for not fully following the regulations prior to the flogging.[23] It was the same Black, 'a good-natured man'[24] who had lent his books to John Mitchel. The bould Thomas Cronin, although wounded twice in the upper body, managed to get over the barrier and was on the quarterdeck when made prisoner. He was serving fifteen years for burglary while his brother James had been transported for life for stealing a gun and firing at a person with intent to kill. Both incidents took place within a few days of each other in October 1846 and the brothers were convicted at the County Limerick Spring Assizes of 1847.[25]

Finally, in September 1855, having served six years out their sentences the four Cappoquin rebels became eligible for release under licence. Under the regulations the prison authorities were required to put them on the first available boat home. Poor James Crotty was ill so only John Donohoe, Luke Lennon and Mathew Joy were discharged from the hulk *Medway*. They came home in style. They were placed on the Bermudan clipper, the *Pearl*, on 8 December 1855 and they reached the Cove of Cork on Christmas Day. The cost of their passages was deducted from their earnings in captivity. There was a short formality of a stay in prison and then home. James Crotty got better and followed them early in 1856.[26] John Donohoe had £9.8s.10d. to show for his time in Bermuda if not a weakened constitution from various periods of illness there. It cannot be said whether his fiancée Bridget Browne waited for him but, if she did, she was soon a widow for he died on 2 May 1858 aged 34. James Crotty fared somewhat better. One source claims that he had served in the British Army and had acted as a drill master for the rebels. He is supposed to have carved his name and address in a Bermudan quarry but it is not known as to whether it still survives there. When he paid for his passage home on the *Castle Eden* his years in Ireland Island left him with £8.5s.2d. He died in Pound Lane, Cappoquin on 30 October 1873 aged 46.

Luke Lennon returned from Bermuda with £8.17s.8d. It is not known whether he resumed his trade as a nailer (a maker of nails) or remained in Cappoquin.[27] Presumably Mathew Joy returned to his family in Carrickbeg. His Bermudan portion was £14.7s.3d. perhaps reflecting the greater earning potential of a spinner. However, technological change and the massive loss of population meant Post-Famine Ireland had less need for spinners not to mention nailers. As regards a return to revolution, further research is needed to discover whether any of the 'Bermudans' joined the Fenians in the 1860s and followed the Green Flag once more.

Notes:

1. Redington to H. Wadington, 20 May 1851, N.A., C.S.O., Gov. Com. Book, 2 January 1849 - 29 December 1851, p. 327; Indent of *Bride*, ibid., G.P.O., C.N. 6, pp.10-17; Journal of J.W. Elliot, P.R.O., Adm., 101/13/4; Gov. Elliot to Earl Grey, 26 June 1851, ibid., C.O. 37, vol. 136, p. 99; Letter to Elliot, 31 March 1851, ibid, vol 138, p. 71.
2. W.B. Johnson, *The English Prison Hulks*, rev. ed., Chichester 1970, p. 166.
3. Kiely, *The Connerys The Making of a Waterford Legend*, Dublin 1994, p. 43; Johnson, op. cit., pp. 158, 172, 176-7, 188.
4. J. Mitchel, *Jail Journal or Five Years in British Prisons*, New York 1868, p. 57.
5. T. Sibeald, *A Sketch of the Bermudas or Somers Islands*, London 1851, pp. 43-4.
6. From 'To George Morgan' in *The Poetical Works of Thomas Moore*, London 1854, pp. 110-11.
7. *Tipperary Free Press*, 14, 17, 21 March 1849.

8. Journal of T.H. Keown, P.R.O., Adm., 101/59/3.
9. Gov. Elliot to Grey, 25 December 1849, ibid., C.O., 37, vol. 128, p. 387; See also pp. 389-90, 393.
10. Ibid., to J.S. Packington, 16 July 1852, ibid., vol. 141, pp. 55, 103.
11. A Field Officer, *Bermuda, A Colony, a Fortress, and a Prison or Eighteen Months in the Somers' Islands,* London 1857, pp. 264-8.
12. *Waterford Mail,* 16 September, 7 October 1848, 10, 14 March 1849; *Cork Examiner,* 20 September 1848; Waterford County Gaol 1848, op. cit; no. 1001; Spike Island Convict Register, op. cit., p. 10; Hulk Registers, P.R.O., H.O., 8, vols. 102 p. 228, 103 p. 231, 104 p. 239, 105 p. 236, 106 p. 216, 107 p. 229, 108 p. 206, 109 p. 208, 110 p. 236, 111 p. 190, 112 p. 211, 113 p. 217, 114 p. 236, 115 p. 208, 116 p. 218, 117 p. 229, 118 p. 235; Ibid., C.O., 37, vol. 144, pp. 228-31, 240.
13. A Field Officer, op. cit., pp. 202-4 claims that there was a plot involving the Bermuda to New York steamer.
14. J. Donohoe & M. Joy, P.R.O., C.O., 37, vol. 147, pp. 119-25. The U.S. fleet under Thomas MacDonough, the great grandson of a Kildare man, won a crushing victory on the Lake at Plattsburgh Bay in September 1814.
15. Ibid.
16. Grey to Murray, 21 December 1854, 29 November 1854, P.R.O., C.O., 37, vol. 148.
17. *Cork Examiner,* 18 September 1848, 23 March 1849; *Tipperary Free Press,* 21 March 1849; Clonmel Gaol Register 1848, N.A., Prisons 1/7/4, no. 2138; Spike Island, op. cit., p. 151; Memorial of Ballyneale & Grangemockler, 6 August 1849, N.A., C.R.F., B8/1851; Hulk Registers, op. cit., vols. 108 p. 160, 109 p. 248, 110 p. 193, 111 p. 225, 112 p. 265, 113 p. 239, 114 p. 260, 115 p. 220, 116 p. 231, 117 p. 239, 118 p. 244, 119 p. 247, 120 p. 255; P.R.O., C.O., 37, vols. 146 p. 341, 151 p. 97.
18. Hulk Registers, op. cit., vol 123 p. 263; C.O., 37, vol. 151, pp. 43, 51, 56; *Cork Examiner,* 14 March 1855.
19. *Tipperary Free Press* op. cit. as above.
20. Memorial of T. Burke April 1849, N.A., C.R.F., B8/1851.
21. See file C.R.F., B8/1851.
22. A Field Officer, op. cit., pp. 211-14.
23. P.R.O., C.O., 37, vols., 127 pp. 237-8, 244, 249, 260, 320; 128 pp. 14, 180-6, 276-9, 289; *Bermuda Herald,* 5 July 1849.
24. Mitchel, op. cit., p. 67-8.
25. *Limerick Reporter,* 9, 12 March 1847.
26. Hulk Registers, op. cit., vols., 126 pp. 302-3, 308; 127 p. 257; N.A., G.P.O., Spike, 624, 656-7/1855; 25, 97, 112/1856; *Cork Examiner,* 28 December

1855, 27 February 1856.

27. See P. Vaughan, *The Last Forge in Lismore*, Dublin 1994, pp. 9-10.

CHAPTER 3 VAN DIEMEN'S LAND & TASMANIA

The seven Cappoquin rebels sent to Van Diemen's Land found conditions there more conducive to their health than their unfortunate comrades in Bermuda. They were brought ashore to the Prisoners Barracks on Hobart's Old Wharf on Christmas Eve 1850. They found a land scarred by the failure of a great social experiment. In the 1840s the Van Diemen's Land probation system was the great hope of penal reform, which would both reform and rehabilitate convicts and also vindicate the whole system of transportation. It was a very complex three-tier system, which involved the classification of prisoners as to their degree of villainy, with strong incentives to progress from the worst to the best and the setting up of a vast network of convict stations. For it to have any chance of success it needed massive capital investment and a highly trained and motivated custodial staff. Needless to say this did not happen and the probation system became a byword for the depths of human degradation.[1] After an official enquiry under Charles Joseph La Trobe the system was soon abandoned. However, as in the best tradition of government policy, it fell on the Governor Sir William Denison to defend transportation during his tenure of office from 1847 to 1854.

For a land the size of Ireland, which in 1851 had only a population of 69,000, the negative image of Van Diemen's Land convicts was nearly matched by their free brethren the sealers and the whalers.[2] Unlike the mainland, there never really was a frontier on the island. The free settlers, mostly of English and Scottish origin, had quickly established themselves on the fertile central and eastern lands and dealt ruthlessly with the small Aboriginal population who as well as being the original occupiers saw sheep as a gift from the landscape.[3] There were bushrangers of course but their cruelty with the possible exception of Mathew Brady and Martin Cash ensured there was never any popular cults as in New South Wales or Victoria. Social mobility was difficult and typical of small societies, origin was remembered.

As the eastern Australian colonies moved towards self government Van

Diemen's Land's free settlers enthusiastically supported inter colonial bodies like the Australasian League and the Anti-Transportation League. In this political milieu the arrival of the seven Young Ireland leaders presented unique opportunities. They brought with them the politics, debates and ideologies of Westminister, the United States and France and consequently many doors were opened to them. However, their followers could not match their high social standing not to mention having difficulties with the English language.

The revolutionary social gulf is best illustrated in the case of two Dubliners, William Paul Dowling and Thomas Fay who were transported for life for their part in the abortive Chartist/Confederate coup in London in August 1848. Dowling was an artist who moved in the highest of London's circles whereas Fay was a boot closer – a person who sews together the leather pattern cut out by another. On their arrival in VDL in late 1849 both secured tickets of leave which allowed them to work freely and earn their living around Hobart. Dowling soon prospered as a portrait painter and was welcome in the highest of colonial society but Fay found the going tough.

The seven Cappoquin rebels arrived a little too late to gain tickets of leave for Governor Denison had imposed a stricter system whereby most convicts had first to become a pass holder before he/she could be considered for a ticket of leave. This effectively ensured that even those with seven year' sentences had to spend up to two years in government service before they could be hired out to the wider community.

John Walsh of Tourin became a pass holder, in May 1852. Sometime early in the following year he went to Nant Cottage in Bothwell, which is about 50 miles north of Hobart and met John Mitchel and John Martin and brought the leaders of 1848 up with the events of 1849.[4] Mitchel later escaped to America but John Martin received a conditional pardon in 1854. This meant that while he could leave Van Diemen's Land he was still excluded from the United Kingdom of Great Britain and Ireland. In his valedictory letter of 12 July, published in the *Hobart Town Mercury* and the *Colonial Times and Tasmanian* he appealed for conditional pardons for eight other Irish political prisoners. As soon as Martin reached Paris, in October 1854, he wrote to the *Freeman's Journal* outlining the fate of the Tasmanian rebels of Cappoquin and William Paul Dowling, 'besides four in Bermuda or some other British penal station' seeking public support for their release. His letter was reprinted in full in the *Cork Examiner* of 30 October and John Francis Maguire, editor as well as M.P. for Dungarvan, corrected a small error where Portlaw was mentioned instead of Cappoquin. It is difficult to assess whether Martin's appeal had any great effect on either the government or public.

However, Maguire did play a leading role in securing the May 1856 pardons for O'Brien, Martin and O'Doherty which allowed them to return to Ireland.[5] In November 1856 the London *Observer* wrote of pardons 'under the Great Seal of Great Britain and of Ireland respectively, to all persons suffering under the consequences of conviction for political offences'[6] but that they would not apply to those who had broken their parole or escaped.

In December the *Dublin Evening Post* which was close to the Liberal government wrote, 'We have learned that a patent has been passed, granting her Majesty's most gracious pardon, and exonerating and discharging from all pain, penalties and forfeitures the following persons'.[7] It then went on to name O'Brien, Martin and O'Doherty, William Doyle and Edward Sheafy (both Portlaw rebels) and all fourteen originally sentenced for the attack at Cappoquin. There was no mention of William Paul Dowling or the fact that William Doyle and John Lennon were long dead.

It appears nothing came of these reports and in October 1857, Terence Bellew MacManus wrote from San Francisco to Maguire saying he wanted no part in the movement to seek pardons for the three American based Tasmanian escapees. MacManus put it bluntly, he would not place himself under obligation to a government he regarded as foreign and as a United States citizen he was free to go where he pleased. However, he was careful to pay tribute to Maguire:

I take the liberty Sir, of addressing this to you, knowing and feeling the warm and manly sympathy you have on all occassions evinced towards us, even in the darkest hour of our adversity, and at the same time beleiving you to be one of the truest and most fearless of Ireland's representatives in that place called the British (not Irish) Parliament.[8]

While it is unclear whether there was any other Tasmanian contact between the rank and file Young Irelanders and the 1848 leadership it is likely that Thomas Francis Meagher knew of their existence. Charles Gavan Duffy wrote to him in September 1850. He took a very critical view of events at Cappoquin and adding '4 or 5 were transported'.[9] Meagher, who thanks to the support of his father, ranks among the wealthiest revolutionaries married a Tasmanian girl, Catherine Bennett. The ceremony at Ross was performed by no less than Dr. R.W.Willson, the Catholic Bishop of Hobart. Meagher escaped from the island to America in 1852. He was collected by boat from Waterhouse Island, off Tasmania's Northeast coast, and landed in Pernambuco, Brazil, from where he reached New York in late May.

Thomas Francis and Catherine were never again to experience their early Tasmanian happiness. Their son Henry Emmet Fitzgerald, born after his father's escape, died of influenza on 8 June 1852 aged four months. His grave can be seen just outside St. John's Church at Richmond. Catherine left the Island and set off to join her husband. She travelled via Ireland and received a tumultous welcome when she visited Waterford City. However, things proved difficult when she rejoined her husband in America. They seperated and a pregnant Catherine returned to Waterford to reside with her father in law Thomas Meagher. She had another son and died there in May 1854 at the age of 22. She is buried with the Meaghers in Faithlegg. Thomas Francis married again this time to Elizabeth Townsend, a wealthy American socialite, but they had no family.

Joseph Brenan celebrated his deliverance in a six-verse eulogy in the *New Orleans Delta:*

To Thomas Francis O'Meagher

Hail, fearless Tribune of an ancient race
Hail, living martyr of a sacred cause!
Unchained, unscathed, thou standest face to face
Triumphant over death and tyrant laws!
A world your forum, and a nation now
Stands 'neath the shadow of th' immortal wreath
That age shall burgeon greenly on your brow;
To see, to hear, to learn with bated breath
Whether their hopes shall bloom again, or wither in inglorious
death.[10]

It is also ironic that the week the "Forty-niners" convict ship reached Hobart, Patrick O'Donohoe's newspaper the *Irish Exile and Freedom's Advocate,* ran an article on a lecture in New York by Joseph Brenan on John Mitchel. Stranger still that O'Donohoe could reprint a speech which was seditious to say the least and which was interrupted by the entrance of the paramilitary Irish Fusiliers.[11] Poor O'Donohoe did run foul of the colonial establishment and after many privations also escaped to America. He got away in 1853, first to Melbourne and then to San Francisco via Sydney. He died in New York on 22 January 1854.[12] William Smith O'Brien who, like John Martin, had received a conditional pardon in 1854 must have known about the "Forty-niners" if only from Martin but he appears to have left it to Martin to seek clemency for them.

O'Brien, Martin and Kevin Izod O'Doherty left to rapturous farewells and public addresses, attended by most of the colony's political and social elite. Some of these functions were well oiled by Irish American funds originally intended to be used for O'Brien's escape. *The Hobart Courier* urged caution in the apparent euphoria about the Irish State prisoners and made the point about the public addresses:

> Nor ought it to go forth to England or Ireland that in this loyal country there are to be discovered any respectable individuals who approve of the treason as well as pity the traitors or who may be esteemed as having been willing to abet the rebellion of 1848, because they have been kind

THOMAS FRANCIS MEAGHER

to the banished authors of it ...to this moment these gentlemen have never expressed any sorrow for the offence which they have committed ... When these exiles have left our shores they will probably never return. They will not, however, have come hither in vain, if they taught the rising generation of this island, that in the present age of the world, the grievances of nations are not to be redressed by the sword of an internecine and a social war. It is by a peaceful, patient, though steady, contest with error, that truth and happiness are eventually to find their sway. If this is an age of opinion, then assuredly we must fight only with the weapons of opinion. Nothing is noble that is not humane, nor is that triumph other than vulgar and barbarous which is stained, in ever so small a degree, by the blood of a fellow citizen.[13]

All the "Forty-niners" eventually secured conditional pardons as did William Paul Dowling, Thomas Fay and three other Young Irelanders who arrived on the island after them – Edmond Sheafy, a painter, of Portlaw, Cornelius Keeffe, a boatman from Carrickbeg and John Shea a labourer from Lisadubber, just outside Carrick, all transported for their parts in the Second Rising of 1848. Unlike the leadership, it appears that most of this group remained on the island even after their sentences had expired. The name Van Diemen's Land did not long survive the arrival of the last convict ship in 1853 and in 1856 it was formally re-invented as Tasmania.

Thomas Wall from Cappoquin, was a sawyer, who was unmarried, aged 24 and able to read a little when he fought for Ireland in September 1849. He was not the first member of his family to go to Australia for his young sister Bridget came out as an assisted migrant to Sydney in the same year. She was with a group of young Cappoquin girls and perhaps the local poor law union may have subsidised their passages.[14] Thomas was a model prisoner in Van Diemen's Land, attending school, working hard for both government and private employers and winning a ticket of leave in February 1854 for his bravery in the disastrous bush fires in the then remote Huon valley, south west of Hobart.

Thomas spent the rest of his life there.[15] He received his conditional pardon in 1856 at Franklin and on 30 April 1857 when described as a

CATHERINE BENNETT

ELIZABETH TOWNSEND

HENRY O'MEAGHER'S GRAVE AT RICHMOND

farmer he married the sixteen year old Hanora Dwyer. Hanora was a Tipperary woman and had come out to Hobart in 1854 with her mother, a sister and two brothers. Thomas and Hanora were married by Fr. John Murphy of Firies, County Kerry, an ordinand of the Missionary College of All Hallows, Drumcondra, Dublin.[16]

It appears that the Irish Catholics in the Huon were very much of Old Ireland as can be seen in the pattern like celebrations, which greeted the opening of St. Mary's Church, at Franklin, on 11 November 1856. The genteel Miss Jane Therry remarked; 'The people of that district are half-savage, and most of them went quite drunk and quarrelled in the presence of the bishop and clergy'.[17]

The tough existence of the Huon settlers has been described as follows:
> The only communication with the outside world was by ship to Hobart town. mainly labourers, ex-convicts and ticket-of-leave men, they only had a few pounds of capital at the most and aimed to subsist until they could clear enough land to produce some surplus. Such settlers scrubbed the land, felled the small trees and cleared the undergrowth during the first years of occupation of the bush. The numerous big trees were ring-barked and left to die. The next stage was logging up, in which bullock teams and hand labour was used to drag logs and branches into heaps for late autumn burning. This continued the second year and with the smaller stumps and roots grubbed out, an effort was made to cultivate a crop, perforce planted between the stumps and standing ring-barked trees.

> During this stage of extremely hard work, muscle-power was clearly king of the economy but there was some compensations in the first crops from rich and virgin soil. Most settlers aimed to clear about ten to fifteen acres to support themselves and their families but in the early stages they were content with a few acres on which they could erect a primitive homestead and plant a kitchen garden.[18]

As well as farming, Thomas Wall as a sawyer, was well qualified to participate in the lumber industry whose greatest resource was *Lagarostrobos franklinii,* the Huon pine.
    During the 1840s, 1850s and 1860s, Huon pining was carried on

extensively in the Huon and Picton rivers, and at Port Davey. It was customary for a couple of piners to row their keelless boat up the river to the forest – the rest of the gang walked. Once there they cut the logs and then felled the scrub to the water's edge. One gang would help another to roll the logs as near as possible to the river bank, and then they waited for a flood to carry them down to Huonville or Franklin. When the flood came, one or two men, according to the size of the boat, followed the logs down to free any that might become stuck in the eddies or racks along the course. The boats were made without keels, and high fore and aft, to allow of them being turned quickly if necessary, on the perilous journey ...[19]

Hand sawing of logs was a most arduous task and for a bottom sawyer it could be hell. His task was to stand in the bottom of the pit over which the log had been rolled and to face the sun and sawdust. It was an exasperated Governor Denison's wish to make a bottom sawyer of Thomas Francis Meagher at Port Arthur should he be re-captured.[20] Needless to say Thomas Wall was a top sawyer.

Thomas and Hanora had a large family of ten boys and two girls and ended up farming 30 acres near the town of Cygnet. They grew potatoes and apples the crops for which the Huon was noted. Thomas died at the age of 69 in 1894 and the death notice inserted in the Hobart *Mercury* said – 'New South Wales & Victorian papers please copy'. He is buried in St. James' Catholic cemetery on the hill up behind the town and there is a headstone. Hanora lived to be 95 and was one of the last surviving pioneers of the district. There is none of the family living there now but the name is still remembered in a field called Wall's paddock on a local farm.[21]

Another of the Cappoquin rebels to end up in the Huon was Thomas Donovan, John Walsh's workman in Tourin. Thomas from Sruh was arrested in 1849 and like most farm labourers of the time could not read or write the English language. He was actually freed in error by the Crown Clerk in March 1850 but he was re-arrested and convicted at the County Summer Assizes. It is not known whether he got any chance to flee the country. He was first attached to a convict work gang, which was based in Hobart's Old Wharf and he duly received his ticket of leave on 8 November 1853. However, he ran into difficulties, perhaps because of

Christmas celebrations and was sentenced to three days solitary confinement on 27 December for being out after hours in contravention of the ticket of leave regulations. Worse followed in August 1854 when he was sentenced to six months hard labour for being 'discovered in having communicated with witnesses under examination'.[22] Thomas was sent to Impression Bay in the Tasman Peninsula but survived to receive his conditional pardon at Hobart in February 1855.

He became friendly with Bridget Lynch, a young Galway girl, and they decided to marry in November 1856. However, as Bridget, was still only a ticket of leave holder permission had to be sought from the authorities; Bridget had arrived in Hobart in February 1853 on the *Midlothian* one of the last convict ships to go to Van Diemen's Land. She had been convicted, with Honora Fahy, at Loughrea Quarter Sessions, in July 1851 of stealing a cow and sentenced to ten years transportation. Her only previous conviction was one month's imprisonment for leaving the workhouse without permission.[23]

Although she was about 22 when she reached the Southern Hemisphere both her parents were dead and her only family was three brothers left at home. Bridget was based at the Female House of Correction, which was at the Cascades, about a mile and a half above Hobart, on the lower slopes of Mount Wellington and worked as a servant for various employers in the town. She was quickly in trouble. In July 1853 she was given seven days of additional probation for being absent without permission. In October when she fled another employer she was given nine month's additional probation on top of nine months hard labour. On 25 May 1854 her son Thomas was born in the Female House of Correction. She declined to name the father. In October 1855 she received fourteen days detention for disorderly conduct. She appears to have left another employer about a week before she received permission to marry and he reported her to the Convict Department. She was officially declared an absconder in the *Hobart Town Gazette* and a reward of ten shillings offered for her capture. The Master and Servants Act which applied in the colony was very severe and weighted heavily towards employers. By the end of November she was reported as apprehended. She had her ticket of leave revoked and was sentenced to three months hard labour but the Governor of Van Diemen's Land had this sentence set aside for her wedding. Bridget was married to Thomas Donovan by Fr. Charles Woods at St. Joseph's Church on St. Stephen's Day 1856.[24]

They soon moved down the Huon valley and by the early 1860s had a hut and ten acres of land at Castle Forbes Bay.[25] Thomas and Bridget eventually ended up at Sandfly, to the east with a holding of 53 acres. Life was difficult for although the Tasmanian economy reached a new peak in 1855 fuelled by the gold discoveries first in California and then in New South Wales and Victoria it then began a slump, which lasted well into the 1870s. Then new mineral discoveries on the island lifted the depression but unfortunately Tasmania had fallen well behind the other colonies to the north.[26]

Thomas Donovan ran into difficulties with the police from time to time because of his drinking and like most of his neighbours he did not see the value of dog licences. However, he had a very strained relationship with his son Peter. Peter, when only eleven years of age, was convicted of stealing twelve loaves of bread in January 1872 and received twelve months in the juvenile house of correction in Hobart. He was sent back later from the Cascades training school and apprenticed to his father. Thomas twice prosecuted him before the Franklin petty sessions for leaving his service without permission and while on the first occasion Peter was sentenced to fourteen days imprisonment on the second he was acquitted because his apprenticeship had expired. Needless to say Peter did not embark on a life of criminality and seems to have been later reconciled with his father. Indeed it may well have been hunger that prompted him to take the bread in the first place.[27] Bridget, 'beloved wife of Thomas Donovan'[28] died at Warwick St., Hobart on 19 January 1883. She appears to have been attending Hobart General Hospital and was buried in Cornelian Bay Cemetery. Thomas Donovan, farmer, died of tongue cancer at Sandfly on 20 December 1884. There is a family memorial in Cornelian Bay, which includes Bridget and Peter who also died in Hobart in 1938 but there is no mention of Thomas who is presumably buried in Sandfly.[29]

There is much less certainty about the fate of the other Cappoquin rebels once they left the convict system. Richard Bryan, Thomas Donovan's work mate at Tourin also ended up in Hobart's Old Wharf. Richard who could read a little had left a wife behind in Ireland. When he was asked on board ship to state his offence as demanded by the regulations he is supposed to have replied,' I do not know what it was for. A policeman died'.[30] Richard progressed quickly through the system and received his conditional pardon at Brighton in September 1854. He was then aged about 32. In July 1857 his seven-year sentence would have expired and he would have been free to return to Ireland. There is a record of a Richard Bryan farming 250 acres at Glenore near Westbury in 1885 but the balance of probability is that it is not the Young Irelander unless the latter became another Antipodean success story

The last of the Tourin workmen Edward Tobin was also married and left behind a wife Ellen. He initially could not read or write but like Thomas Wall became a zealous attender at school. However, the indulgence gained here was more than offset by the award of three months additional probation for laziness in February 1852. Soon after he became a pass holder and went to work in the Oatlands district in the Midlands. He seems to have celebrated the Nativity of 1852 in some style for he was sentenced to three days solitary confinement for being in town without permission. He duly received his ticket of leave the following Christmas but ran into trouble in August 1854 when he was sentenced to three months hard labour for 'gross misconduct in enticing a female pass holder from her services'.[31] In February 1855 he was fined the enormous sum of £1 for being drunk in Westbury. He received his conditional pardon at Circular Head in the Northwest in August 1855. It may be that he was working for the Van Diemen's Land Company, a much smaller version of the East India Company, which had extensive land holdings in that area and had imported many farm labourers from Ireland. In August 1857 Edward sought fit to request a certificate from the Convict Office that his sentence had expired and this was sent to Morven.

An Edward Tobin was a tenant farmer on 50 acres at Sassafras for most of the 1860s, 70s and 80s. During this time what has been described as 'all cold, damp, black forbidding with huge tall trees standing erect like a phalanx of warriors that were masters of the situation was tamed and brought into cultivation'.[32] This Edward had a wife Anne Murphy and their son Michael's birth was registered in the Deloraine district in 1860. A daughter Johanna died in 1868 when she was accidentally burned a few months short of her sixth birthday. It may well be the same Edward, a farmer aged 57, who married an Anne Fogarty (sic), a [Military] Pensioner's widow aged 45, at St. Patrick's Church Latrobe in 1876. In the early 1890s this Edward and Michael were farming at Barrington described as 'fine agricultural country and settled by a superior class of farmers'.[33] Finally, Edward died of heart disease at Sherwood on 19 December 1898. On the death certificate his place of birth is given as Ireland and his age 80 years suggests he may well have been the Cappoquin rebel.

John Walsh, the farmer, who had led out his workmen to battle like a Gaelic or Highland chief is unlikely to have been abandoned by his family in Ireland. As well to do farmers they would have been in a position to send some help. Although no petitions were sent on his behalf to the Government it is interesting to speculate whether any unofficial approach was made using clerical channels. Whatever the case John appears to have had no problems with the convict system and while a pass holder, went to work for John Regan in Liverpool St.

Regan, a Corkman, was a prominent Hobart merchant, who had done well in the wool and leather business. He was a significant Catholic layman who donated the massive sum of £1,000 to St. Joseph's Church.[34] It appears also that he represented Thomas Francis Meagher and his father in financial matters and perhaps the relationship was similar to that of the other Hobart Irish leather merchant Isaac Godfrey Reeves with William Smith O'Brien.[35] In addition John Regan offered his home to Patrick O'Donohoe when the Young Irelander first arrived in Hobart. O'Donohue who is contrast to the other six leaders had no private resources and set up the *Irish Exile and Freedom's Advocate* primarily as a means to earning a living.[36] Similarly, John Mitchel spent many hours in Regan's fine house Laburnum Park, just outside Hobart. Indeed Regan was more that willing to help all Irishmen:

> During the whole of his long residence in Hobart Town he seemed to be impelled with a zeal for doing good, especially to his unhappy countrymen who arrived in the colony as convicts. Many a young Irishman he saved from moral destruction by procuring for him proper industrial employment, and by exercising over him the tender care of a second father. Indeed next to the faithful Irish Priests of Tasmania, John Regan may be called the providential guardian of the Irish convicts of the Settlement.[37]

John Walsh began working for Regan in May 1853 just as an Irish American sponsored rescue attempt took shape. In July 1848 Patrick James Smyth together with Philip Gray had made an abortive attempt to spread the rebellion in County Meath. Smyth, who had been at school with Meagher at the Jesuit Clongowes Wood, later escaped to America. He earned the nickname Nicaragua for his vigorous campaign, in the pages of the *New York Sun* against British interests in Central America. Smyth arrived in Hobart in January 1853. He eventually succeeded and helped Mitchel to escape in July while at the same time escorting Mrs. Jenny Mitchel and the children to Sydney.

Smyth fell deeply in love with Jeanie, 'the tall handsome dark-eyed girl',[38] and daughter of John Regan, who looked after him when he was seriously ill and laid low for about two months. He seems to have proposed to her. Smyth was sent back once more in 1854 by the American Irish to liberate the three remaining Young Ireland leaders, William Smith O'Brien, John Martin and Kevin Izod O'Doherty but his arrival coincided with their receipt of conditional pardons. Bishop R.W. Willson officiated at his marriage to Jeanie in St. Joseph's Church on 8 February 1855.[39]

It is interesting to speculate whether John Walsh had any dealings with Smyth and whether John's visit to Nant Cottage was anyway connected with the Mitchel rescue. John Walsh received his ticket of leave in November 1853 and secured a conditional pardon at Westbury in September 1854.[40] His life thereafter remains a mystery but it seems unlikely that he ever returned to Tourin.

The fate of James Casey, the weaver from Clonmel is also unclear. He was single aged 30 and could read a little when arrested in September 1849. For some reason he was classified in the convict records as a labourer but when his real trade was discovered he was transferred to the Weaver's Shop in the Cascades factory in July 1851. He seems not to have killed himself with work and in the following year he was given three month's additional probation for idleness. In 1853 he had a spell of employment with Charles Giles, a Hobart boot and shoemaker and then went north to work for the magistrate and politician Alexander Rose. Rose, a Scot, had greatly expanded the land holdings and livestock interests of his uncle who was originally granted Corra Linn the family property.[41] Routine and hard work may soon have dimmed the beauty of the gorge and cataract, which had given Corra Linn its name but James Casey would have no difficulty in appreciating the apt use of Gaelic. In 1811 it had been so named by Lachlan Macquarie the famous Governor of New South Wales while on a journey from Hobart to Launceston. The home of William Wallace, the great Scottish hero was his inspiration.[42]

James Casey was still in this district, Morven, when he received his conditional pardon in October 1855. In 1872 a letter was received in the Hobart Post Office enquiring for James. They passed it on to the Convict Department but he could not be located. His relative Catherine Johnson of Dungarvan sought him in vain.[43] It maybe that he was resting in a Launceston cemetery since 1867. On 7 October 1862 a James Casey, labourer, aged 42, married Ann Harrison in Launceston's York St. Baptist Chapel. A James Casey, labourer, aged 44 (sic), died at Launceston on 10 December 1867.

The family of James Lyons, the last of the Cappoquin rebels in Van Diemen's Land made every effort to save him. His mother Mary, an aged widow, with a large family, had protested his innocence in a petition to Clarendon, the Lord Lieutenant. It appears she ran some kind of a shop in Cappoquin and had barred the door when she heard gunshots on the fateful night. She said James was inside when the attack took place and remained there until breakfast the following morning. Her daughter Anastasia and son Michael confirmed the alibi and a neighbour Catherine

Cleary, who had come to the house for some new milk, was certain that James was inside with his family while the Young Irelanders fought on the street outside. Mrs Lyons explained the post trial introduction of Catherine Cleary by saying she had not been heard before, as it was thought not necessary. There was also the dubious identification of John Brien who not alone had placed James Lyons at the barracks but also gave him a pike in his hand. Mrs. Lyons stressed that at the trial Judge Pennefather had remarked that Brien the approver was also an accomplice.[44]

The petition was not successful, however, and Judge Pennefather was satisfied with the jury's verdict so James found himself working with the others on Hobart's Old Wharf. James, a farmer, in Ireland was classed as a labourer in Van Diemen's Land. In May 1852 he made a major change in profession when he became a special constable at Ross over 70 miles north of Hobart. This career should have received a major setback in November when he was dismissed and sentenced to two months hard labour for being discovered in making a false statement. Yet in the following January he was appointed a constable in the Convict Department and may still have been in that capacity when he received his conditional pardon at Port Arthur in August 1855.[45] Needless to say the convict policeman looms large in the history of policing in New South Wales and Van Diemen's Land with a perceived legacy of corruption and indiscipline. The public, naturally, were slow to trust them and of course their fellow convicts hated them. However, the authorities were unable to do without them. If James Lyons took the job as an easier means of passing his sentence he would also be aware how dangerous it was as well as the possible repercussions of meeting people who had completed their sentences. With the ending of transportation to Van Diemen's Land in 1853 and the processing of the existing convict population the island's penal system contracted rapidly so it is unlikely that James served as an ordinary policeman in the new Tasmania.

Although he had a sister Mary in America and could have gone there immediately – money permitting or returned to Ireland in 1864 after his sentence expired; it seems likely he spent most if not all of the rest of his

JOHN MITCHEL   JOHN MARTIN

NANT COTTAGE 1996

life in Tasmania. A James Lyons was farming on Pipers River in the 1880s and at Turners Marsh in the 1890s he had a cottage and 75 acres. This man died of heart disease in the Launceston General Hospital on 29 January 1898. His age at death 70 would make him the same as James of Cappoquin.

Only poor health has prevented Edmund Sheafy from accompanying William Doyle to Bermuda in 1849.[46] Sheafy from Portlaw has received ten years transportation for his part in that attack on that barracks during the Second Rising of 1848. His petition to the government failed the same as William Doyle's although their co-defendant the blacksmith James Kenna, President of the Owen Roe Confederate Club in Carrickbeg, had a similar sentence reduced to eighteen months.[47] Sheafy, a painter, had a wife Mary and four children. By 1851 he was deemed fit enough to survive a sea voyage and at 2.00 p.m. on 29 July he sailed on the *Blenheim* with 309 other convicts from Queenstown. He distinguished himself during the voyage as an infirmarian (medical orderly) and received a special recommendation from the Surgeon. The moral and religious instructor on board was Fr. Charles Woods who was on his way to join the Hobart mission. In August 1847 Bishop R.W. Willson visited Irish seminaries seeking recruits. In All Hallows, Dublin, a priest and three students including Woods volunteered. He also persuaded another three students in St. Kieran's Kilkenny and a priest and deacon in St. John's Waterford to opt for the Southern Hemisphere.[48] Now an ordained Woods, from the parish of Munterconnaught, Co. Cavan, was travelling to his diocese at British Government expense. In his journal he wrote of the convicts dancing on deck and four deaths; two convicts, one guard and a child, which marked the passage. He 'observed many among the prisoners who are very ignorant of Christian doctrine & who could not well understand English. Got another prisoner who understood the Irish to instruct them in the Irish Cathecism'.[49] Unfortunately he did not name this prisoner. On the morning of Halloween 1851 the *Blenheim* reached Hobart. Procedures required that all details of each prisoner be registered by the Convict Department staff, before any were landed so it was a week later before everyone was ashore.

Edmund Sheafy was attached to a gang at the Cascades factory and by the end of August 1852 he was allowed into private service as a pass holder. He worked for various employers in Hobart and duly progressed to his ticket of leave. Christmas appears to have posed problems similar to some of the other Young Irelanders and just after the Epiphany of 1855 he was sentenced to seven days solitary confinement for being out without his pass. However, he received his conditional pardon at Hobart the following April. He was then about 36 years of age and would be free to return to Ireland in March 1859 when his sentence expired.[50] Despite having a very rare surname he appears to have left no traces on the island. Maybe he eventually managed to return home to Mary and the children.

If Edmund Sheafy fought at Portlaw on the morning of 12 September 1848 in the afternoon Cornelius Keeffe saw action at Rathgormack. He was with a band of rebels under John Dee of Ballindysart who demanded the firearms of James Hahassy at Aughmore. Dee had two farms and lived close to the chapel of Windgap, 'the bell of which ringing is the precursor of every insurrectionary movement in this party of the country'.[51] Hahassy and his two sons refused to hand over their weapons and a confused standoff developed in a field outside the house. Thomas Hahassy and John Dee squared up to each other apparently to fight a duel but this quickly developed into a melee involving the Hahassys and their farm servants and the rebels in which Dee shot and wounded James. James Hahassy recovered from his injuries, John Dee could not be found by the authorities but Cornelius Keeffe of Boherbue, Carrickbeg and Martin Callaghan of Amber Hill, Kilmeaden were arrested and charged with appearing in arms.[52] At the County Waterford Spring Assizes for 1849 they pleaded guilty and were sentenced to seven years transportation.

While both maintained they had been forced to join the rebels, only the campaign to reduce Callaghan's sentence was successful. It helped that he was only eighteen years of age and that his employer the magistrate Richard Thomas Barron of Sarah Ville, Kilmacthomas was convinced of his innocence. His sentence was commuted to two years imprisonment in December 1849. Cornelius Keeffe was a Carrick boatman, a member of

TASMANIA 1889

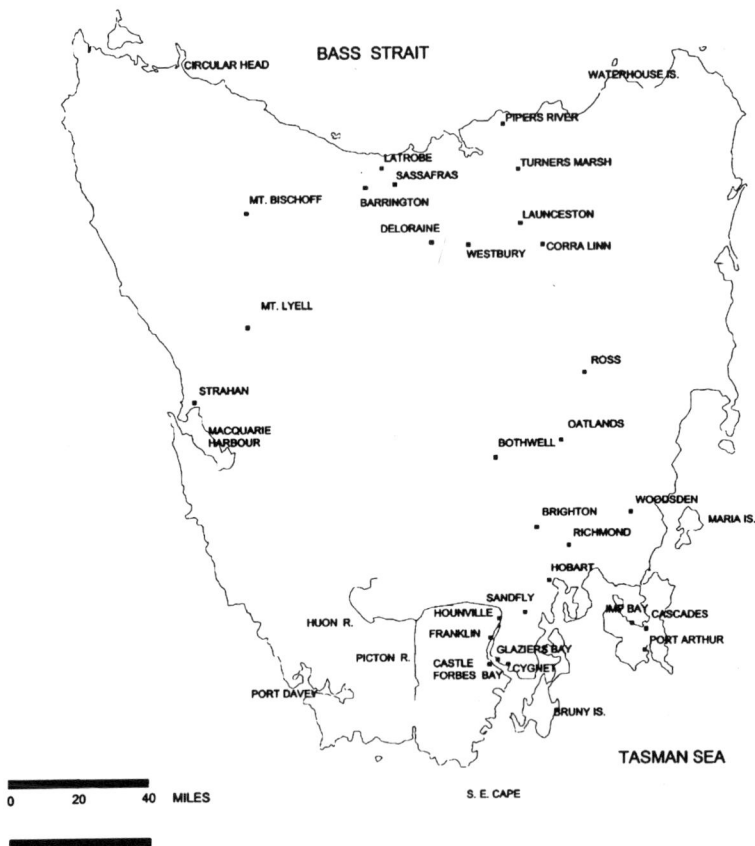

CIRCULAR HEAD

BASS STRAIT

WATERHOUSE IS.

PIPERS RIVER

LATROBE
SASSAFRAS
TURNERS MARSH

MT. BISCHOFF
BARRINGTON
DELORAINE
LAUNCESTON
WESTBURY
CORRA LINN

MT. LYELL

ROSS

STRAHAN

MACQUARIE HARBOUR
OATLANDS
BOTHWELL

WOODSDEN
BRIGHTON
RICHMOND
MARIA IS.

HOBART

SANDFLY
HOUNVILLE
HUON R.
FRANKLIN
PICTON R.
CASTLE FORBES BAY
GLAZIERS BAY
CYGNET

IMP BAY
CASCADES
PORT ARTHUR

PORT DAVEY

BRUNY IS.

TASMAN SEA

| 0 | 20 | 40 | MILES |

S. E. CAPE

Tasmania 1889

a cohesive organised group who had made their presence felt in industrial and political matters for generations. However, they were now under severe pressure from the great industrialists the Malcolmsons of Portlaw who were determined to control freight rates on the Suir. Cornelius 'was a very poor man'[53] approaching middle age and supporting a wife and a cousin's two orphan children when he was arrested. The other Carrick boatmen did the best they could to help his family but conditions were dire.

The first memorial submitted on his behalf in April 1849 had the signatures of all the local Catholic clergy, the Vicar of Carrick, the Mayor of Waterford and Nicholas Foran, Bishop of Waterford & Lismore. This tone is very different to the petitions on behalf of Martin Callaghan:

> He sincerely repents the late mistaken course he has taken but was carried away by the excitement of the times and the unparalleled distress and destitution which reigns in this locality, the want of food and absence of employment. Seeing himself and neighbours perishing daily and no hopes held out to them to better their condition forgetting himself and thinking his deplorable state could not be worse he is now suffering the penalty of his indiscreet conducts and throws himself on your Excellency's mercy.[54]

It went on to express serious concerns about his health if kept in gaol or transported. However, the surgeon in Waterford County Gaol when he examined Keeffe reported to the government, 'I am of opinion that his life is in no danger whatsoever, having a couple of boils on his left forearm …'[55]

In September 1849 Cornelius Keeffe sent his own petition to the Lord Lieutenant explaining that his employer for the last sixteen years was willing to take him back and looking for some reduction in his sentence. Finally in January 1850 his clerical backers made an effort to get the government to extend the clemency shown to Martin Callaghan. The memorial described Keeffe as being tried for a 'political offence'[56] and requested the Lord Lieutenant not to 'leave him alone the only political convict now in the County Gaol of Waterford'.[57] It is unlikely that Dublin Castle were impressed given that they were just finalising prosecutions against the Cappoquin rebels and Cornelius Keeffe's file was closed with, 'let the law take its course'.

In May 1850 he was sent to Spike Island Prison and finally on 30 April 1852 he sailed on the *Lord Dalhousie* bound for Hobart. Although Cornelius could neither read nor write English his correspondence address in the Spike records is given as wife Johanna c/o Jas. Kina (sic) Carrickbeg.[58] By this time the Portlaw rebel James Kenna had finished his sentence. *The Lord Dalhousie* first called to Kingstown Harbour and embarked some convicts and then came down the east coast and across to Queenstown and eventually had 324 prisoners on board. She was the first Irish male convict ship for 1852 and had Fr. John Murphy as religious and moral instructor for the Catholics with W.A. Tully looking after the Protestants.[59] The voyage took 105 days and deaths included two children and three military pensioners but three babies were born on board. These would be with the families of the convict guard. Cornelius Keeffe was deemed fit for employment and one week later, on 21 August 1852 he set foot on Van Diemen's Land.[60]

He was immediately allowed into private service and went to work for Rev. John Andrewartha, a Church of England missionary chaplain and entrepreneur, in the Huon district. It appears that Rev. Andrewartha allowed secular matters to dominate his life and he resigned in March 1853 just as enquiries were about to be made into his business affairs. He was later supposed to have gone to New Zealand and taken up survey work.[61] Cornelius was back in the Prisoners Barracks in Hobart in May 1853 and in December of the following year he received his conditional pardon. In March 1856, when he was about 48 years of age he applied for a certificate that his sentence has expired and perhaps immediately afterwards set out for Ireland and Carrickbeg.[62]

In the meantime, Bishop R.W. Willson had sent Fr. John Murphy, his All Hallows recruit, to Norfolk Island a beautiful Pacific island with a fearsome reputation.[63] The Bishop had been appalled when he visited in 1852 and saw the regime administered by the notorious Governor Price.[64] Fr. Murphy remained ministering to the convicts until 1855 when Norfolk

Island was rapidly being run down as a prelude to closure – a casualty of the ending of transportation to Van Diemen's Land. It closed in early 1856 and the remaining convicts were removed to Port Arthur. They were replaced by Pitcairn Islanders.[65] In March 1855 the Bishop sent Fr. Murphy to Franklin in the Huon Valley where for over 40 years he performed an excellent ministry.

The last Young Irelander of all to be transported was the labourer John Shea of Lisadubber outside Carrick-on-Suir. He sailed from Queenstown on the *Lord Auckland* on 29 September 1852. Along with Thomas Burke and William Kelly he had been sentenced to ten years transportation for attacking Glenbower barracks in September 1848. The local clergy interceded with the Lord Lieutenant on his behalf and one of the memorials bears the signature of James Hackett Mandeville of Ballycurkeen House, brother-in-law of John O'Mahony – but to no avail.[66]

John Shea was in Mountjoy Jail in December 1850 when a Mr. Dease of 7 Upper Thomas St. sought clemency for the prisoner 'in the beautiful prison beside me! under condemnation of transportation for ten years for nothing'.[67] Dease in his slightly idiosyncratic letter to Sir Thomas Redington, the Under Secretary explained that John Shea has been a devoted servant for fifteen years to a very young widow, Mrs. Ryan, with an only child a beautiful daughter of about fifteen or sixteen years. He wrote of how John had married Mrs. Ryan's favourite maid and the couple had been given a cottage on their employer's land and that he had just rented some land from his mistress. Dease maintained that John was working at fencing a pasture on the day Glenbower barracks was attacked. However, John and some companions did go out one night to capture some small songbirds, linnets, robins and wrens, to amuse the children including young Miss Ryan. Dease explained, 'The times were angry; Smith O'Brien & Meagher pursuing their wild projects the signal fires just quenched, in that wild and mad district Tipperary'.[68] Three policemen came to Mrs. Ryan's and arrested John in the garden just as he was about to put a bird into a bag. John was released on bail to appear before the magistrate Henry Briscoe – a week later.

However, Dease claimed that John's brother William indignant at the turn of events 'said partly to himself partly about; heck there were little matter that ass broke its neck before it arrived at the chapel'[69] as he watched a policeman's wife ride to Mass that Sunday.

At the hearing before Briscoe three policemen swore that John was at Glenbower.

Dease then claimed that things went from bad to worse at John's trial at the Tipperary Spring Assizes of 1849. He had no legal representation and called no witnesses and was distracted by the fact his wife was about to have their first baby and pleaded guilty because he was persuaded by "an artful witness"[70] that it was necessary to save his life.

Dease wanted the innocent man re-united with his wife and the infant he had never seen. In a powerful concluding passage he wrote:

> Dear, dear, Sir uphold the privilege of our lovely young Queen – uphold the glory of the British constitution – equal liberty to all her Majesty's loyal British subjects – uphold humanity, truth & justice and graciously give me the great happiness of sending John Shea, to his own fireside, to his beautiful young wife, his innocent infant & let it be remembered that the reign of Clarendon, was the reign of truth – vertue and religion.[71]

Needless to say this did not happen and John Shea for reasons which are unclear was not sent with the other Glenbower men to Bermuda or dispatched earlier to Van Diemen's Land. His ship the *Lord Auckland* suffered two convict deaths and after a voyage of four months John and 245 others arrived at Hobart in January 1853.[72]

Like Cornelius Keeffe he was immediately made a pass holder and went to work for the landholder Thomas Cruttenden of Woodsden, Prossers Plains. John seems to have soon decided that his fortune lay in Tasmania for in April 1854 his application for a passage for his wife and family was recommended. Bringing out the families of transportees was a long-standing British government policy designed to both populate the colonies and rehabilitate the convicts by restoring them to the mediating influences of family life. In September he received a ticket of leave for the Richmond district and seemed to be progressing smoothly through the system. However, on 15 June 1855 he was absent from his residence and drinking with some others on White Marsh sheep station when poor drunken John Riley, a 40 year old labourer shot himself with a loaded gun. He died from his injuries three days later. John Shea received three months hard labour in the Prisoners Barracks, Hobart for his presence at the tragedy and was not allowed to return to live in the Richmond district. However, this was no longer relevant when he received his conditional pardon in January 1856.[73] A John Shea farmer and native of Tipperary died of influenza at the Landsdowne Crescent, Hobart residence of his son-in-law on 13 October 1894. His wife Alice died two years later and both rest under a headstone at Cornelian Bay cemetery.[74]

As mentioned earlier Irish revolutionaries in England had two representatives in Van Diemen's Land. In the crisis of the summer of 1848 the English Confederate Club network attempted to supply arms to Ireland and the same time were drawn into ambitious plans for an English revolution. This centred on a joint Chartist/Confederate attempt to seize power in London on the evening of 16 August 1848. William Paul Dowling and Thomas Fay were on the crucial organising committee, which met in various London coffee houses and public houses to organise the coup. However, the Government, thanks to the their agent the carpenter Thomas Powell alias Johnson were well aware of their deliberations. It is ironic that at the last meeting of the committee Thomas Fay and another were delegated to investigate Powell who had come under suspicion.[75] By the afternoon of Wednesday 16 many of the leaders were in custody and troops were on full alert at Buckingham Palace, the Tower, the Royal Mint, the Bank of England and various other key points.[76] Thomas Fay aged 22 was arrested in his father Patrick's house, at 14 Plough Court, Milton St. and brought straight to Bow Street.[77]

Fay's position as secretary both of the Irish Felon Club and a Chartist Club, which met in Cartwright's coffee house Red Cross St., brought him on the organising committee. The Irish Felon Club has been an ordinary

Confederate Club but had changed its name to show its support for John Mitchel when he was expelled from the Irish Confederation in 1847. The better off social strata of the London Young Irelanders were in the Davis Club and they were loyal to the Smith O'Brien leadership and committed to working within the law. However, the secretary Francis Looney received two years for sedition under the Treason-Felony Act for a speech on 8 July 1848. A new secretary, William Paul Dowling, events in Ireland and a visit from Michael Doheny, 'a wild Irish ruffian'[78] tilted the balance towards physical force. Dowling was invited on to the organising committee and apparently charged with Fay and others with raising the Irish contribution of 5,000 men to the revolution. Dowling was arrested by the police on Lambeth Walk on 20 August.[79]

At his committal hearing in Bow St. Fay seemed to a reporter to be 'a poor simple fellow'[80] who while admitting that he was a delegate at various meetings claimed that he did not know what this entailed. At his trial he said that he resigned both offices of secretary on the Saturday before the 16th. At the Old Bailey in September Dowling was charged that he did with others 'compass, imagine, devise and intend to levy war against the Queen ... with intent to depose the Queen from the style, honour and dignity of the Imperial Crown'.[81] The prosecution was led by the English Attorney General. Dowling was defended by the Cork barrister Edward Kenealy, a former president of the Davis Club who had resigned on the issue of physical force. Dowling's statement before examining magistrates was recalled at the trial, 'I do not wish to stand here as an English factionist but as an Irish nationalist, my object was not to disturb English society, but to free my own country'.[82] He was found guilty and sentenced to transportation for life. Edward Kenealy, who was not known for modesty, felt he had given Dowling a good defence and in admiring the Attorney General's technical skill wrote: 'to be sure he had a packed jury and a packed bench, and a host of witnesses who traded in perjury; but still his conduct of a difficult prosecution deserves the praise of dexterity'.[83]

Fay and Dowling spent a year in London's Millbank and Newgate Prisons before the *Adelaide* brought them to Van Diemen's Land. In the meantime many more Chartists were convicted and sentenced to transportation. It was claimed by the authorities that an essential part of the planned rising in London and the three great industrial cities of Manchester, Liverpool and Birmingham was wide scale arson.[84] In Liverpool an arms supply to Ireland network based upon the Sarsfield Club was broken up. One of the main leaders Dr. Lawrence Reynolds of Waterford City escaped to America but his assistant in the arms shop at 110 Leeds St., Joseph Cuddy, and eight others received sentences ranging from two years to three months.[85] It is unlikely English public opinion could have stomached death sentences for those involved in the events of 16 August. Similarly, it should never be forgotten that Victoria's great popularity dates from the later part of her long reign. Once the non capital punishment strategy was adopted against the Chartists and their Irish Confederate allies it followed that Whitehall would not allow the death penalties handed down on the Young Ireland leaders at Clonmel to be confirmed. Even had there been no English attempt at revolution William Smith O'Brien's status as an M.P. would have dictated extreme caution. As it was the British Government was able to pursue a policy of comutation of death sentences in Ireland and when it deemed that the maximum had been gained from the strategy sanction the official announcement of the royal reprieves in the summer of 1849.

Thomas Fay had no difficulties with the penal system in Van Diemen's Land and in February 1857 together with Dowling he received a full pardon. Therefore, he was no longer excluded from England or Ireland. However, he chose to remain in Tasmania. He never again regained the prominence he had for that short period in London and he did not come to the notice of John Martin who sought clemency for the Dowling and the seven "Forty-niners". In December 1865, at Launceston, Fay was sentenced to three months hard labour for illegal pawning and at Hobart the following May he was convicted of stealing a carpet and got one month.[86] There are no more details on his Tasmanian convict record. He ended his days in New Town Charitable Institute a haven for many ex-prisoners, where he died on 25 March 1898 aged 72 years. He was buried the following day in a pauper's grave in Cornelian Bay Cemetery.[87]

In contrast William Paul Dowling, the son of a solicitor, prospered in portrait painting and photography. He was able to have his fiancée brought out from Dublin and although there was a slight hiccup when he had his ticket of leave revoked in March 1853 for missing a muster he quickly got it back when he explained his absence.[88] While it appears that Dowling had finished with revolution the day he left the Old Bailey there surely is a certain symbolism in his portrait of Richard Dry. Here was a Young Irelander painting Dry a prominent Tasmanian politician and Speaker of the Legislative Council but also son of a Wexford Protestant United Irishman who was transported for life to New South Wales in September 1797. Dowling did return to Dublin for a short period but decided his future lay in Tasmania where he died in 1877.[89] Irish influence on Tasmania was never great and once transportation to the Island ended and the Young Ireland leaders departed it declined from a temporary high. Richard Dry, the Tasmanian Irishman, born at Elphin station near Launceston, did achieve a knighthood and was a very successful premier from 1866 to his death in 1869. However, his political career was issue based centring on opposition to transportation, Australian federation and northern railway development.[90]

Tasmania finally began to pull out of the economic slump caused by the ending of transportation and the collapse of Antarctic whaling when tin was discovered in the west at Mount Bishoff in 1871. Discoveries of gold and the giant copper field at Mount Lyell in 1883 created a mineral boom. However, this did not fuel much Irish immigration. Yet the Irish community at Hobart remained significant enough to be courted by any Irish political leader on an Australian tour.

Patrick James Smyth with Jeanie by his side was certain that Tasmania was the finest part of Australia when he lectured the Catholic young men of Waterford City in 1861:

Tasmania, the gem of the Australian colonies, and as fair an island as any the sun Looks down on. The climate is pronounced to be the finest in the world: sufficiently cold in winter to make vigorous outdoor exercise desirable, and a blazing wood fire in the hearth pleasant in the evening; in summer hot, but not oppressively so. It seemed to me to be perfection. As a consequence of this incomparable climate, the land in

PATRICK JAMES SMYTH M.P.
WESTMEATH 1871-79, TIPERARY 1880-82

this island is richer and better adapted for agriculture than in any of the colonies of the mainland.[91]

Indeed Smyth drew attention to the fact that Ireland lagged way behind the other island in terms of political development:

In saying farewell though, to this loveliest island, I would ask you to reflect on the fact that, with a population of not quite 90,000, she possesses a parliament of her own, with a constitution larger by far and more liberal – therefore designed to endure – than that which Grattan and the Volunteers won for Ireland in 1782.[92]

The nineteen Young Irelanders sent to Tasmania were but a tiny fraction of the estimated 14,492 Irish born men and women who ended up as convicts in Van Dieman's Land.[93] Thus there was never the concentration of this political group as occurred with the United Irishmen in New South Wales at the start of the century. Indeed, the United Irishmen's last battle was in March 1804 at Vinegar Hill o'er the River Hawkesbury. In contrast although there was some contact between the exiled July 1848 leadership and those rank and file transported for subsequent revolutionary activities it appears that no attempt was made to forge a Tasmanian Young Ireland organisation. Rather it was personal contacts and the American Irish, which brought about the escape of four of the leadership. The rest of the leadership and the other twelve Young Irelanders eventually achieved freedom under the convict system. There was never a question of them being an exempted group which is what provoked John Devoy and the American Irish to launch the *Catalpa* rescue of Fenian military convicts from Western Australia in 1876.[94]

Notes:

1. See I. Brand, *The Convict Probation System: Van Diemen's Land 1839-1854*, Hobart, 1990.
2. In the census of 1 March 1851, 20,069 out of 69,187 were returned as the Convict Population. *Statistics of Van Diemen's Land 1844-1853*, Hobart 1854.
3. M. Cocker, 'The last Tasmanian', *Independent on Sunday* (magazine), 26

April 1998 pp. 10-13, W. Denison, *Varieties of Vice-Regal Life,* vol 1, London 1870, p. 67; Kiely, The Connerys, op. cit., p. 86.

4. Cavanagh, Meagher, op. cit., p. 217.
5. Davis, pp. 323-4.
6. Carried in *Cork Examiner,* 12 November 1856.
7. *Dublin Evening Post,* 17 December 1856.
8. *Cork Examiner,* 7 December 1857.
9. C.G. Duffy to Meagher, 13 September 1850, in T.J. Kiernan, *The Irish Exiles in Australia,* Melbourne 1954, p. 93.
10. First of six verses in *Munster Advertiser,* 17 July 1852.
11. *Irish Exile and Freedom's Advocate,* 14 December 1850.
12. See R. Davis, 'Patrick O'Donohoe: Outcast of the Exiles', in B. Reece ed., *Exiles from Erin Convict Lives in Ireland and Australia,* Dublin 1991, pp. 246-83.
13. *The Courier,* 11 July 1854.
14. See Appendix 5 Emigrant Girls.
15. Waterford County Gaol Register 1849, op. cit., no. 1373; A.O.T., Con., 33/100, no. 23,757; Index of *Hyderabad* (3), Con., 14/43; Index to Conditional Pardons, Con., 56/3, no. 1,224; *Colonial Times,* 14, 17, 24, 28, January, 2, 8,11 February 1854; *The Courier* 13, 14, 16 January 1854.
16. Marriages in the District of Huon, A.O.T., 37/1857/506; Hanora's family came on the *Northumberland* which sailed from Southampton on 9 April 1854 arriving in Hobart on 25 July 1854. They were claimed by their brother William, who was already in the colony. See C.B., 7/16/1, p. 88; C.B., 7/15/1 & C.S.O., 24/252/10266 & M.B., 2/39/18, p.179. See also K. Condon, *The Missionary College of All Hallows 1842-1891,* Dublin 1986, p. 296.
17. W.T. Southerwood, *Planting a Faith in Tasmania, The Country Parishes,* Hobart 1977, p. 142.
18. L. Robson, *A Short History of Tasmania,* Melbourne 1986, pp. 30-1.
19. A. McMullen, 'Timber and Sawmilling', *Huon and Derwent Times,* Huon Centenary Settlement, December 1936.
20. Denison, op. cit., p. 182.
21. *The Mercury,* 31 August 1894, 9 January 1936; Tasmania Deaths District of Port Cygnet 1936, 1894. Fr. John Murphy celebrated the first regular Masses in Cygnet in a house rented from a Mrs. Wall (sic) for £10 a year, Southerwood, The Country Parishes op. cit., p. 145. Wall's Paddock (1996) is on the farm of Martin Brereton near enough to Glaziers Bay. In 1869 Thomas Wall had applied to Government for 20 acres of Huon land in the parish of Leithbridge and Thomas Donovan for 50 acres in the parish of Honeywood. See A.O.T., L.S.D., 1/80, pp. 283-4. Waterford County Gaol

Register 1849, op. cit., no. 1369; ibid., 1850, Prisons 1/39/4, no. 797.

22. A.O.T., Con., 33/100, no. 23,562; *Hyderabad* Indent, Con., 14/43, p. 43; Con., 56/3, no. 1454.

23. Galway County Gaol Registers of Tried & Untried Prisoners 1851, N.A., Prisons 1/21/3, no. 1492; 1/21/4, no. 184 (from Spring to Summer Assizes). Both girls were committed to gaol by the magistrate John W.H. Lambert of Aggard, Craughwell.

24. *Midlothian* Indent, A.O.T., Con., 15/8, p. 27; ibid., 41/36, no. 546; Permission to marry, 52/7, p. 97; *Hobart Town Gazette* 18, 25 November, 2 December 1856; Register of Marriages in the District of Hobart 1856 & Register of Births 1854.

25. Valuation Roll, District of Franklin 1862, p. 4.

26. Wapping History Group, *'Down Wapping' Hobart's vanished Wapping and Old Wharf Districts,* Hobart 1988, pp. 53-4.

27. Court of Petty Sessions Franklin, 24 April 1868 to 30 May 1895, A.O.T., L.C., 282/1, pp. 8, 131, 182, 186, 196, 261, 275, 284, 288, 449, 501, 515.

28. *The Mercury,* 20 January 1883. See also Register of Deaths Hobart 1883; Valuation Roll, District of Franklin 1884.

29. Register of Deaths Franklin 1884; Valuation Roll, Franklin 1884 in *Hobart Town Gazette,* 27 November 1883, p. 1523; *The Mercury,* 3 June 1938.

30. Indent of *Hyderabad,* op. cit., no. 23,508; 14/43, p.13; 56/3, no. 1190. See also Waterford County Gaol Register 1849, op. cit., no. 1374; Valuation Roll, Westbury 1885 in *Hobart Town Gazette,* 27 January 1885, p. 197.

31. *Hyderabad* Indent, op. cit., no. 23, 744; 14/43, p. 103; 56/3 no. 451; Waterford County Gaol 1849, op. cit., no. 1368.

32. J. Fenton, *Bush Life in Tasmania Fifty Years Ago,* reprint Launceston, 1989, p. 111.

33. Ibid., p. 182.

34. J.H.Cullen MS, Tasmanian Library, p. 30.

35. Kiernan, op. cit., pp. 99-100; See also R. Davis ed.,*'To Solitude Consigned' The Tasmanian Journal of William Smith O'Brien 1849-1853,* Sydney, 1995.

36. Cullen (book), op. cit., p. 114.

37. Death of a Worthy Irishman, *Irish Citizen,* 12 December 1868.

38. See Smyth to O'Doherty, 17 August 1853, in Kiernan, op. cit., pp. 119-20; L. Smyth Griffith, Memoirs of the late Mr. P. J. Smyth M.P., N.L.I., MS 4758, chp. V, p. 5.

39. Southerwood, The Convict's Friend, op. cit., p. 157.

40. *Hyderabad* Indent, op cit., no. 23,758; 14/43, p. 109; 56/3, no. 1400; Waterford County Gaol 1849, op cit., no. 1373.

41. See David Rose & Alexander Rose, A.O.T., Wayne Index.

42. See J. Taylor & J. Smyth, A Dictionary of Tasmanian Place Names, work in progress 1993, in Tasmanian Library; Kiely, the Connerys, op. cit., p. 71.

43. *Hyderabad* Indent, op. cit., no 23, 530; 14/43, p. 21; 56/3, no. 810; Waterford County Gaol 1849, op. cit., no. 1324.

44. See James Lyons, N.A., C.R.F., L26/1850.

45. *Hyderabad* Indent, op cit., no. 23,646; 14/43 p. 63; *Hobart Town Gazette*, 16 November 1852, 11 January 1853.

46. Spike Island Register, op. cit., p. 10.

47. Unable to locate E. Sheafy's Convict Reference file i.e. C.R.F., S9/1849. Kenna's file K2/1850 is attached to the files of T. and J. Ryan R28/1850. See also N.A., O.P., 29/134/1849; Waterford County Gaol, op cit., 1848 no. 926, 1849 no. 201.

48. Southerwood, The Convict's Friend, op. cit., p. 74.

49. Journal of C. Woods, A.O.T., Con., 76/1.

50. *Blenheim* Indent, A.O.T., Con., 33/104, no. 24,892; 14/42 p. 271; 56/3, no. 402.

51. *Waterford Mail,* 27 September 1848.

52. See Martin Callaghan, N.A., C.R.F., C62/1849; Cornelius Keeffe, K3/1850; Waterford County Gaol 1849, op. cit., nos. 45, 144.

53. J. Clarke to Rennison, 30 April 1849 in C.R.F., K3/1850.

54. Keeffe, ibid.

55. James Cavet, 10 April 1849, ibid.

56. Keeffe, ibid

57. Ibid.

58. Spike Island Register, op. cit., p. 99.

59. N.A. G.P.O., CN 6, p. 47.

60. Journal of C.A. Anderson & *Lord Dalhousie* papers in Returns from Irish Convict Ships, M.L., FM 4/3132.

61. J. Andrewartha, Wayne Index, op. cit.

62. *Lord Dalhousie* Indent, A.O.T., Con 33/109, no. 26,247; 14/45, p. 81; 56/3, no. 1292.

63. Southerwood, The Convict's Friend, op. cit.

64. R. Hughes, *The Fatal Shore,* London, 1988, pp. 549-50.

65. C.M.H. Clarke, *The Earth Aludeth for Ever 1851-1880. A History of Australia,* vol. IV, Melbourne, 1980, p. 106.

66. Memorial of J. Shea, 13 April 1849, N.A., C.R.F., B8/1851.

67. Dease to Redington, 9 December 1850, ibid.

68. Ibid.

69. Ibid.

70. Ibid.

71. Ibid.
72. C. Bateson, *The Convict Ships 1787-1868*, Glasgow 1985, pp. 370-1, 394.
73. Clonmel Gaol 1848, op. cit., no 2183. See *Lord Auckland* Indent, A.O.T., Con., 33/112, no. 27,211; 14/32, p. 229; Inquest on J.Riley, ibid., S.C., 195/36, no. 3538.
74. *The Mercury*, 15 October 1894.
75. J.D.Barnet & A. Bucker, *Central Criminal Court Session Papers*, vol. XXVIII, London, 1848, p. 810.
76. *The Times*, 17 August 1848.
77. Barnet & Bucker, op. cit., p. 829.
78. A. Kenealy, *Memoirs of Edward Vaughan Kenealy*, London, 1908, p. 119.
79. See Barnet & Bucker, op. cit., pp. 728-45.
80. *Cork Examiner*, 21 August 1848. See Barnet & Bucker op. cit., p. 792.
81. Barnet & Bucker, op. cit., p. 728.
82. Ibid., p. 751.
83. Kenealy, op. cit., p. 121.
84. Barnet & Bucker, op. cit., p. 852.
85. M. Cavanagh, *Waterford Celebrities*, Waterford, 1900, pp. 3, 15; See The Times 22, 24 August 1848; *Cork Examiner*, 18 December 1848; See Appendix 3 - Prisoners for rest of names.
86. *Adelaide* Indent, A.O.T., Con., 2/364, no. 1673; 14/38, p. 217.
87. Register of Deaths in the District of Hobart 1898; Cornelian Bay Burial Register, no. 1B 11457, A no. 259.
88. *Adelaide* Indent, op. cit., no. 1672; 14/38, p. 217.
89. A. Mac Lochlainn, 'William Paul Dowling Letters of a Transported Felon', lecture at Ninth Irish-Australian History Conference, Galway 1997. See also R.Davis, 'Unpublicised Young Ireland Prisoners in Van Diemen's Land', in *Tasmanian Historical Research Association Papers & Proceedings*, vol. 38, nos. 3 & 4, December 1991, pp. 131-7 and G. Rudé, *Protest and Punishment, The Story of The Social and Political Protestors transported to Australia 1788-1868*, Melbourne, 1978, pp. 80, 100, 144, 218-9, 255-6 for other views on the lesser known twelve Young Irelanders.
90. See *A.D.B.*, vol. 1, Melbourne, 1966, pp. 329-30.
91. P.J. Smyth, *Australasia A Lecture delivered before the Catholic Young Men's Society of Waterford*, 2nd ed., Dublin, 1861, p. 21.
92. Ibid, p. 22.
93. J. Williams, *Ordered to the Island Irish Convicts and Van Diemen's Land*, Sydney, 1994, p. 158. The 14,492 were composed of 4,637 women and 9,855 men. Kiely, The Connerys, op. cit., p. 103 has estimated the numbers of convicts sent directly from Ireland to N.S.W. at 27,000 (5,000 women and

22,000 men) almost twice the Tasmanian figure. Con Costello puts the total of Irish Convicts sent to Australia as 45,000 in his Botany Bay, Cork, 1987, p. 9. The grand total of Convicts sent to Australia (1788-1868) is put at nearly 160,000 comprising over 78,000 to New South Wales, over 65,000 to Van Diemen's Land and close to 10,000 to Western Australia in J.C.R. Camn & J. McQuiston eds., *Australians: A Historical Atlas*, Sydney, 1987, p. 200.

94. See S. Ó Lúing, *The Catalpa Rescue*, re-issue of *Freemantle Mission*, Dublin, 1985 and K. Amos, *The Fenians in Australia 1865-1880*, Kensington N.S.W, 1988, pp. 200-57.

CHAPTER 4 THE GREEN FLAG

After the failure of September 1849, James Fintan Lalor returned to Dublin. His health, which had never been too robust, finally broke down and he died on 27 December. He was buried in Glasnevin Cemetery. Philip Gray also back in Dublin attempted to keep the '49 movement going but by 1850 it was obvious even to him that it had no future. He returned to ordinary life and got a job in an office in Smithfield. As for Thomas Clarke Luby he was still unsettled and in the autumn of 1851 he decided to join the French Foreign Legion. However, when he arrived in France he found that the Legion was no longer recruiting. He spent another year in Ireland and then left for Australia.[1]

If the Irish revolutionaries were demoralised in the early 1850s then they were only reflecting the deep malaise in society as a whole. Even the Catholic Church experienced a crisis of confidence. The great expansion in church and school building had been severely curtailed by the Famine. The Church had also lost its great ally Daniel O'Connell and worse still during the spiritual questioning and uncertainty a number of priests had defected to the Established Church. It was also under pressure from well-financed attempts by Protestant Evangelicals to bring about a new Reformation in Ireland. Moreover, the conduct of the British government during the Famine has sown a deep distrust even among the Bishops. Thus, there was a certain inevitability about the formal condemnation of the Queen's Colleges in 1850 by the Synod of Thurles and, even more so about the setting up of the Catholic Defence Association of Great Britain and Ireland in August 1851 to combat the new Ecclesiastical Titles Act. This Act restricted the titles that could be assumed by Catholic Bishops. In particular it was designed to ensure that among the recently restored English hierarchy there could be no Catholic Archbishops of Canterbury or York. Many Catholics saw the Act as heralding a new wave of persecution against the Church, which in the worse possible scenario would see all gains since Emancipation in 1829 overturned. While this did not happen it was only the passage of time which made it clear. It was well into the 1850s before the Irish Catholic Church began to recover and undertake its own reconstruction. Only then did Paul Cullen's attempts to reshape and modernise the institution in a more Roman image really begin to succeed.

There was to be no comeback for the Irish language upon whose speakers, death and emigration in the seven years from the autumn of 1845 fell heaviest. Now even the old heartlands of West Ulster, Connacht and Munster appeared vulnerable to linguistic change. Yet Irish was still useful as a political medium and remained very much a language of dissent. At an election meeting in Dungarvan in July 1852 Fr. Michael O'Connor displayed his fine radical pedigree and mastery of oratory in Irish. He had been a leading tithe activist in the 1830s and widely suspected by the authorities of the day of helping the notorious Connery brothers. He was greatly respected for his efforts to relieve distress during the Famine and was a strong supporter of the Tenant Right Movement:[2]

> The Rev. Mr. O'Connor of Kilgobinate (sic), addressed the meeting, in Irish, in a strain alternatively jocular and serious, and with a fancy versatile and flexible as the glorious old tongue in which he spoke, and depicted the baneful effects of English power in Ireland. He denounced in wrathful terms the blasphemous impiety of those who attribute the Irish Famine to the Almighty, as they were merely artificial the result of Whig and Tory robbery and mismanagement. If a single stalk of that unfortunate esculent (sic), the potato, had never grown in Ireland, the Rev. speaker affirmed that there was sufficient quantity of the best food grown in the country to support double its population. He introduced several simple and appropriate parables, a la Fontaine to illustrate his views, amongst the rest a very expressive one, in which he represented the Whigs and Tories as rival communities of cats and dogs who contended with each other for the exclusive privilege of devouring the mice (the people) which each considered its legitimate prey.[3]

In that general election about 40 Irish members were returned in the Tenant League interest. Fr. Richard Walsh C.C. (John's brother) came to the attention of the authorities for an address he gave at Cappoquin. He was also prominent in defending his parishioner Mr. Bronogue (Brennock) who was convicted at the town's petty sessions of assaulting the magistrate Christopher Ussher of Camphire at the polling in Lismore.[4]

JAMES FINTAN LALOR

Brennock a small farmer from Sruh in the Knockmealdown uplands challenging a magistrate brought home once more the vulnerability of the hold of the gentry on the Irish countryside.

Similarly, the loyalty of the police, in the face of the Young Ireland threat in 1848 and 1849 did nothing to improve their popularity among wide section of the community. Although the military occupation of Cappoquin ended in the autumn of 1852 and the garrison at Ballinamult was also withdrawn a police detachment was still stationed in the Mothel house of Rev. Hill, which had been attacked by the rebels during the Second Rising of 1848. In October 1852 Civitas in a letter to the *Waterford News* denounced the Carrick police whom he/she believed were useless for preventing crime being only interested in corrupting local women:

> Nearly all our street prostitutes have been first ruined by the police. There are three of the force "protecting" a Protestant Parson, at Mothel, since '48, and they have bastardised that that locality so much that they were denounced from the altar of the Parish, by the Catholic Curate, the Rev. Mr. Fogarty [C.C. Clonea & Rathgormack]. What does Colonel M'Gregor [Inspector General of Constabulary] think of this immoral conduct?[5]

The women of Cappoquin had been protected for most of the military occupation by the Sisters of Mercy who arrived in the town from their convent in Wexford in answer to an urgent plea from Fr. Spratt P.P.

Thomas Clarke Luby sailed from Liverpool on the Dutch barque *Mathilde* on 29 October 1852. There was an 8 day stopover in Rio de Janeiro, a call to the Dutch East Indies and they reached Melbourne on 6 April 1853.[6] Like many he prospected unsuccessfully for gold and then crossed Bass Strait to spend some months in Van Diemen's Land. It is not clear what exactly he was doing there or whether he made any attempts to contact the Young Ireland rebels. Similarly, whether he was on the Island or back in Victoria for the celebrations which greeted the release of William Smith O'Brien, John Martin and Kevin Izod O'Doherty in July 1854. All he says himself is that he was back again in Dublin in the fall of 1854 having been away 'some days over two years'.[7]

It may be the purest of coincidences but William Smith O'Brien's triumphant progress through Geelong, gold mining Bendigo and Melbourne could not but have helped to harden the resolve of Irish diggers at Ballarat. There frustrations over a primitive licensing system, the absence of political representation and disgust at the perceived corrupt administration of justice provoked a miner uprising which was crushed with the capture of the Eureka Stockade early on Sunday morning 3 December 1854. Their leader Peter Lalor, James Fintan's brother, had his left arm 'shot off'[8] as he led a vain defence. It is tempting to make comparisons with New South Wales in 1804 and to regard Eureka as Young Ireland's Victorian Castle Hill. However, while Peter Lalor a civil engineer had emigrated to Australia in 1852 with his brother and two sisters and had inherited his family's radical tradition he was certain that his notion of democracy did not include Chartism, Communism or Republicanism.[9] Certainly all these political philosophies had their adherents among the leadership and the multinational mining community at Eureka but the majority like Lalor settled for a redress of their grievances and an improved parliamentary democracy.

Meanwhile, the Crimean War (1853-56) embroiled the empires of Britain, France and Turkey against that of Russia and galvanised Irish American revolutionaries. John Mitchel and later John O'Mahony sought military assistance from the Tsar's government but to no avail. However, some consoled themselves with the prospects of a crushing British defeat. This euphoria helped to launch the *Tribune* in Dublin on 3 November 1855. Its message was uncompromising '...Only in the regeneration of an Irish Nation is there any hope for the general mass of people ... The *Tribune* shall defend the principle of nationality against all its foes'.[10] Needless to say Thomas Clarke Luby was one of the sub-editors and Philip Gray was involved on the office side. Although it claimed to have the support of the Irish American leaders it only ran for fifteen issues with the last appearing on 15 February 1856. Luby blamed its demise on mismanagement by Thomas Mason Jones the owner and editor but optimistic views on international relations which discerned the demise of the British Empire, war between the United States and Britain and Russian victory in the Crimea did not help the paper's credibility. Philip Gray well used to disappointments now began to attend lectures on chemistry at the Museum of Industry in St. Stephen's Green. He was in poor health since he burst a blood vessel on St. Patrick's Day 1855 and had difficulty in earning a living. He spent part of the summer of 1856 in Meath with his relatives but was unable to arrest his physical decline. The end came at 9 Lombard Street where he first lost his speech and finally just before midnight on 25 January 1857 'the pallor of death suddenly overspread his face – sudden as shadows passing over grass or water – and he breathed his last'.[11] Gray was aged 35. Luby has left the following description of his friend:

> ... About 5 feet 6 inches high and of slender make. He had small and beautiful hands. His frame was wiry and capable, until his constitution was impaired by disease, of enduring fatigue and hardship to a degree scarcely credible. He was activity. He would appear in places distant from each other in the shortest time ... He told me that he couldn't look on a common street row without feeling an uncontrollable excitement. He was sometimes in manner a little a little irritable and bitter. His Celtic looking face especially indicated his nervous temperament. His complexion was fair, his hair light brown. He had singular eyes ... Indeed, he had naturally an admirable turn for humour ... His talk was wholly free from humbug, affectation and cant. His habits and manners were generally retiring. In conclusion, Gray was a man unique.[12]

Luby with other of his old friends and Philip's brother John ensured that he was buried according to his wishes beside his father in the family burial place of Kilglass just outside Longwood in County Meath. They brought the remains by train to Enfield and were joined by the relatives, friends and sympathisers, as they walked the coffin to Kilglass. Luby spoke at the graveside. At his side was James Stephens. Both would later establish the Fenian Movement in Dublin on St. Patrick's Day 1858 and John O'Mahony would spread it in America.

It was the same John O'Mahony who in 1857, in New York, published *Foras Feasa ar Éireann,* Seathrún Céitinn's seventeenth century historical masterpiece, which much to his regret served as an epitaph for Old Ireland.

JOHN D. HEARN

With the death of Brenan at New Orleans in the summer of 1857 Luby
was now the last surviving member of the leadership of 1849. He used his
legal studies to draw up the Fenian oath and just as he once accompanied
James Fintan Lalor he went with Stephens on a recruitment drive through
the Irish countryside. John O'Mahony slipped back to Ireland in the
winter of 1860 to review progress. He was accompanied by John D.
Hearn, the Dungarvan leader, in 1849. Hearn, over six feet tall and a fine
athlete was very steady and cool. No sooner had he come to America in
1850 that he was involved with Brenan in Irish military organisations in
New York and naturally he became a Fenian. He remained in Liverpool
when O'Mahony returned to the United States.[13] The new organisation
pulled off a major coup in America and in Ireland by bringing home the
body of Terence Bellew MacManus back from San Francisco for burial
in Glasnevin Cemetery. MacManus was the first of the Young Irelanders
to escape from Tasmania and managed to get away on a ship from
Launceston in March 1851.[14] While the body was lying in state in Dublin,
in November 1861, an attempt was made by what the Fenians considered

to be a Young Ireland faction to take over the ceremonies but Luby and the American delegation saw them off. A clerical boycott collapsed when Archbishop John McHale of Tuam allowed Fr. Lavelle officiate at the graveside and the crowd at the funeral was said to be bigger than that which said the last farewell to Daniel O'Connell.[15]

However, the organisation was still small and would never manage to integrate its open American wing with the undercover and secret Irish organisation. In February 1863 Luby was dispatched to America by Stephens to raise funds and to ensure John O'Mahony followed the directions of the Kilkennyman. Luby travelled widely but ended up with little money and diplomatically avoided the quarrel between O'Mahony and Stephens.[16] He also met John Hearn who had thrown up a good job in Liverpool to join the staff of Thomas Francis Meagher's Irish Brigade. Hearn, a captain in the 164th New York Volunteers of the Corcoran Irish Legion, was captured at the Battle of Ream's Station, Virginia on 25 August 1864. The precarious nature of the American organisation can be judged by the fact that O'Mahony and his secretary Michael Cavanagh believed they were in some danger of being drafted by the Union army. O'Mahony felt he was safe on the grounds of age but if the worse came to the worse Cavanagh was willing to go on the run. However, O'Mahony was recognised as being important to the Union war effort and was later made a colonel so the danger receeded.[17]

By war's end the exploits of Irish units including the Irish Brigade, on the Union side, made Irish emigrants more acceptable to Americans. The Fenian organisation in America had become stronger and created an army and naval force but in 1865 neither Stephens nor O'Mahony were able to organise an uprising in Ireland. Incidentally John Hearn, who had survived his Confederate prison, was one of the Irish American officers who returned home to prepare for action. Dublin Castle and Whitehall were well briefed by agents at the heart of the movement. In September 1865 in a raid on the influential Fenian newspaper the *Irish People* the police arrested Luby, the owner, Jeremiah O'Donovan Rossa, the manager and John O'Leary, the editor all key elements in the leadership. In November even Stephens was arrested although he managed to escape from Richmond Gaol and reach France. On this occasion there was no quick release for Luby; he was convicted of Treason Felony and sentenced to 20 years penal servitude. He experienced the harsh regime of Pentonville and later Portland while his wife Letitia did her best to keep her husband's situation in the public eye. It would be January 1871 before he got out of prison, his freedom and that of 32 others helped in no small way by a broadly based amnesty campaign. However, freedom came at a price namely that the unexpired period of the Fenians sentences be spent in exile. Luby first went to Belgium with John O'Leary and he was re-united with Letitia and the children in Antwerp. The Lubys stayed there a few weeks and then left for America.[18]

Meanwhile, in America, O'Mahony in order to bolster the issuing of Fenian bonds gave into pressure to create an administration in waiting. However, as President he was unable to control his Senate or Cabinet or prevent the strategy of freeing Ireland by way of Canada gaining ground. Like all political emigres the Irish revolutionaries risked being sucked into the domestic concerns of the host country as expansion to the north had at least occupied American minds as much as the move westwards. O'Mahony tried to sideline the Canadian option by attempting to seize a small island called Campobello off the Maine/New Brunswick coast in dispute between Britain and the U.S. but this turned into a fiasco.

By late May 1866 the Fenian Secretary of War ordered an invasion of Canada and deployed forces from St. Albans in Vermont to Michigan. On 2 June at Ridgeway, Ontario the forces of John O'Neill carrying a green flag emblazoned with a golden harp and the initials I.R.A. defeated the British army/Canadian militia and retreated in good order to the United States border.[19] O'Neill, a native of Drumgallon, near the Monaghan/South Armagh border, was a resourceful Civil War veteran who had served with the U.S. Cavalry and as Captain of the 17th United States Colored Infantry. In the frost and snow of March 1867 the Fenians Irish rising soon petered out. John O' Mahony who with Michael Cavanagh celebrated in verse the departure of arms, officers and ammunition on the Fenian *Erin's Hope* were bitterly disappointed. It was all over even before the ship had left New York Harbour on 13 April. In

JOHN O'MAHONY

Donegal Bay, on receipt of intelligence, the plan to take Sligo town was quickly abandoned and they set sail for the south coast. Nearly all those who came ashore in Ring, Co. Waterford on 1 June were quickly captured although they had the foresight not to land the supplies which were brought back to America.[20] In the end the Fenians even with their professionalism and better military training achieved little more than the efforts of the Young Irelanders in 1848 or 1849.

Luby, back in America in 1871, where he would spend the remaining 30 years of his life, had to get used to a Fenian organisation where O'Mahony and Stephens had long been yesterday's men. Luby and the other recently freed leaders tried to unite all the different factions but to no avail. John O'Neill, who had launched an unsuccessful assault on Canada from Franklin, Vermont, the previous year, on 5 October 1871, in defiance of the rest, seized the Hudson's Bay Company post of Pembina in Manitoba's Red River Valley. It now even became obvious to him that the strategy was a failure not least because of the growth of Canadian Nationalism following Confederation in 1867.[21]

Luby's status earned him a place on the Skirmishing Fund set up by Jeremiah O'Donovan Rossa in 1876 but its very inception was testament to the realities facing a small revolutionary organisation. However, Luby's heart was no longer in it and it was only loyalty to and concern for his friend John O'Mahony that kept him active. O'Mahony was confirmed as titular head of an ostensibly united Fenian organisation just before his death in 1877. Luby was one of the chief pallbearers at the New York ceremonies, which took on all the trappings of a state funeral. The burial in Ireland was equally impressive and clerical hostility was more than countered by the Bishop of Cloyne allowing a low Mass for the remains in the Pro-Cathedral at Queenstown.[22] O'Mahony was laid to rest beside MacManus in Glasnevin Cemetery giving himself in death to the political movement which had dominated his life for as Luby pointed out O'Mahony wished to be buried 'beside his mother in the old Munster grave of his fathers'.[23]

Luby left the Fenian brotherhood soon after O'Mahony's death. In 1878

THOMAS CLARKE LUBY

he published the *Lives and Times of Illustrious Irishmen* to complement his 1872 biography of O'Connell and when he wrote to Charles Gavan Duffy in 1881 he stated 'I am now out of all Irish-American movements'.[24] Needless to say Luby 'denounced the dynamite party and abhorred all incitement to assasination'.[25] He continued with his writing and the *Story of Ireland's Struggle for Self Government* of which he was the chief contributor was published in New York in 1893.

Luby's reputation for accurate recollection of events during his long revolutionary career ensured that he was consulted by Duffy and John O'Leary as they prepared their historical works. This together with his own journalistic work has ensured that he has helped to shape our understanding of the period. He died at the age of 80 in Jersey City on 29 November 1901.[26]

Notes:

1. T.C. Luby, N.L.I., MS 332, p. 25
2. Kiely, The Connerys, op. cit., p. 34; *Cork Examiner*, 14 February 1849; W. Fraher, B. Sheridan, S. Ó Loinsigh & W. Whelan, *Desperate Haven, The Poor Law, Famine & Aftermath in Dungarvan Union*, Midleton, 1995, p. 25; Scéal Tomás Ó Corcoráin, P. Ó Milléadha eag., 'Seanchas Sliabh gCua', *Béaloideas*, iml. VI, 1936, lch.199; Scéalta Liam Ó Caoimh & Séan Ó hAirt, N. Breathnach eag., *Ar Bóthar Dom*, An Rinn, 1998, lcha. 125, 162-3.
3. *Munster Advertiser*, 10 July 1852.
4. Rev. Mr. Walshe's adddress at Cappoquin, rec. 7 July 1852 (index entry only) in N.A., O. P., 1852 – unable to locate file 29/153.
5. *Waterford News*, 15 October 1852.
6. Luby, MS 332, op. cit; M.A., Syme, *Shipping Arrivals and Departures, Victorian Ports* Vol 2, 1846-1855, Melbourne 1987, p. 159.
7. P. Lalor to R. Lalor, 4 June 1855, in Kiernan, op. cit., p. 148. See also, J. Molony, *Eureka*, Ringwood Vic., 1989.
8. Kiernan, op. cit., p. 149.
9. *The Tribune*, 3 November 1855.
10. See *Irish News*, 14 March 1857 & *Irish Nation*, 17 June 1882.
11. *Irish News*, ibid.
12. Ibid.

13. See Cavanagh, Meagher, op. cit., pp. 17-18; D.P. Conyngham, *The Irish Brigade and its Campaigns,* L.F. Kohl ed., New York, 1997, pp. 481, 490-1; Luby, *Irish World,* 24 March 1877.

14. Kiernan, op. cit., p. 110. See J. Denieffe, *A Personal Narrative of the Irish Revolutionary Brotherhood,* reprint Shannon, 1969, pp. 64-71.

15. Ibid., p. 154.

16. Denieffe, op. cit., pp. 77-9; Luby, *Irish World,* 24 March 1877; *Dictionary of National Biography Twentieth Century 1901-1911,* Oxford, 1989 ed., pp. 485-7; O'Leary, op. cit., pp. 207-26.

17. M Cavanagh to O'Mahony 31 July/ 2 August 1862, Catholic University of America, Fenian Brotherhood Records 1855-1910, Box 2.

18. O'Leary, op. cit., pp. 107-8, 111, 129-30; T.C.Luby to L. Luby, 12 January 1871, in *Cork Examiner,* 16 January 1871.

19. See H. Senior, *The Fenians and Canada,* Toronto, 1978, pp. 99-106; *Dictionary of Canadian Biography Vol X 1871-1880,* Toronto, 1972, pp. 558-9; Battle of Ridgeway, C.W. Desperate Charge of the Fenians under Col. O'Neill near Ridgeway Station June 2 1866 and total route of British Troops, including the Queen's Own Regiment under command of Col. Booker. Print, Buffalo N.Y., 1869 in National Museum of Ireland. Canada West (C.W.) became Ontario in 1867.

20. J. De Courcy Ireland, 'Fenianism and Naval Affairs', in *Irish Sword,* vol. VIII, no. 30, Summer 1967, pp. 11-12; Senior, op. cit., pp 119-21. Feach freisin ar N. Ní Mhuirí, 'Teacht na bhFinin go h-Eilvic 1867', N. Breathnach eag., *History, Lore & Legend through the eyes of the Young,* Waterford, 1987, lcha. 52-3.

21. Senior, op. cit., pp. 132-4.

22. *Irish World,* 10, 17, 24 February; 3, 10, 17, 24 March 1877.

23. T.C. Luby, ibid., 14 April 1877.

24. Luby, MS 332, op. cit., p. 26.

25. K. Luby Maurice to Col. Moore, 22 June 1926 attch. N.L.I., MS 331. Feach freisin ar S. Ó Lúing, *John Devoy,* Baile Atha Cliath, 1961, lch. 64.

26. S. Ó Lúing, Introduction to Denieffe, op, cit., p. x. Thomas Clarke Luby's MS 331 of 1 September 1891 & MS 333 of 20 April 1892 were written for John O'Leary and MS 332 of April 1881 was written for Charles Gavan Duffy.

CHAPTER 5 EPILOGUE

The failure of 1849 was Young Ireland's last attempt at revolution. Three efforts in Ireland together with a joint operation with the English Chartists clearly shows that the Young Irelanders did not fail for want of trying. In spite of the chaotic and disorganised nature of Smith O'Brien's Rising it still required a major effort by the authorities to defeat it. The Second Rising of 1848 was a much more determined affair and for a few short hours O'Mahony's forces caused panic until the various reverses caused the revolt to collapse. 1849 was the most professional of all and the elaborate preparations mark it as beyond a mere amateurish operation. While it did not achieve success it was rightly seen by Dublin Castle as a serious attempt to overthrow the Union.[1] 1849 also witnessed the complete transformation of the open organisation of the Confederate Clubs into a secret society. Similarly, the 1849 leadership was much more radical than the group around Smith O'Brien. This radicalism together with the mode of organisation would be very evident in the Fenians who had many '49 men both in the leadership and ranks.

It seems also reasonable to suppose that only death deprived a Fenian leadership of the services of Philip Gray and Joseph Brenan. However, had Brenan lived longer it is interesting to speculate whether his support of the American South and defence of slavery would have been as extreme as that of John Mitchel. Mitchel whose opinion of convicts deteriorated rapidly as he left Bermuda for Van Diemen's Land was also one of the fiercest opponents of Reconstruction the process whereby the Federal military occupation of the South was used to extract and enforce civil rights for the freed slaves.[2] As regards Tasmanian Fenians there was plenty of potential recruits in Hobart and down the Huon Valley but much research still needs to be done on the movements presence on the Island. Unfortunately this study was unable to discover anything on the subsequent political affiliations of the Irish Tasmanian "Forty-niners" Thomas Wall and Thomas Donovan. However, suffice to say that the arrival of Fenian prisoners in Western Australia in 1868 and subsequent escapes and the shooting of Alfred, Duke of Edinburgh in Sydney in

MONUMENT TO THOMAS FRANCIS MEAGHER 1905

March of the same year ensured that Australians could not but be aware of the movement's existence. Indeed they greatly impressed the Irish Australian outlaw and rebel Ned Kelly who includes them in his famous Jerilderie letter.[3]

In stressing the importance of 1849 in the evolution of Irish revolutionary movements mention must be made of the inspiration drawn by the participants from the United Irishmen. That there were family links is not surprising given the sheer scale of casualties in the former movement. Joseph Brenan's grand uncle died a soldier's death in 1798. He could even have been killed at the battle of Ballinascarthy in West Cork given that Brenan's family had links with Skibereen. Philip Gray had a grand uncle in Co. Meath who was hanged by the yeomen perhaps after the battle of Clonard. John O'Mahony's father and uncle were active in the United Irishmen and either may have been the Mr. Mahony who was to command Glenahiery in North West Waterford in the abortive rising of September 1799. It also seem likely that John D. Hearn of Dungarvan was related to Francis Hearn, an ex-clerical student who was executed for his part in the same attempt to raise South Tipperary and West Waterford. September 1799 also claimed the life of the legendary Éamonn Paor but the other main leader Philip Cunningham of Moyvane and Clonmel was sentenced to trasnportation for life. He subsequently perished in New South Wales, at Vinegar Hill oe'r the River Hawkesbury leading the United Irishmen in their last battle in March 1804. Michael Cavanagh tells us that it was from his neighbour, an elderly woman, that he discovered that a grandfather was a United Irishman.[4]

The Young Irelanders appear not to generate much interest among Irish academics and most of the modern historical scholarship has been Australian and United States based. The great interest generated by the anniversaries of the Famine and 1798 has barely touched the Young Irelanders. This limited field is naturally dominated by Smith O'Brien and the men of '48. James Fintan Lalor still commands sporadic interest as a political thinker but the rest of the '49 leadership is long forgotten. In 1926 when Katharine Luby Maurice presented her father's papers to the National Library she underlined this fact when she wrote 'Please do not think that I exaggerate my father's importance or feel any bitterness at the obscurity into which his memory has fallen'.[5] In 1940 against the backdrop of a renewed I.R.A challenge to the De Valera and British Governments the veteran republican, poet and writer, Brian Ó hUiginn attempted to resurrect Philip Gray as an ideal role model. In his *Wolfe Tone Annual* he appealed to the men of Meath to find Gray's grave.[6] It is not known whether this resulted in any commemoration ceremony at Kilglass but it certainly did not produce a headstone. Today, the spreading tree under which Gray was buried no longer exists and his final resting-place still remains unmarked. Yet it may be that the Irish State's purchase of the Widow McCormack's house in 1998 will help to revive interest in the men and women of 1848 and 1849.

If 1849 finished Young Ireland for good it also ended any hope of recovery for Old Ireland. John O'Mahony's deep commitment to the Irish language is underlined in the way he uses the ancient scribal tradition to end his English translation of Foras Feasa ar Éireann:

> *Ar na chríchnúghadh i g-cathair Brúcluinne, laimh re h-Eborach Nuadh, le Séaghan Mac Domhnall, Mhic Thomás Oig na bh-Foradh Ui Mhaghthamhna ó Choill Bheithne, laimh re Sliabh Grott ris a radhter an Ghaillte Mhor aniu, ar an t-ochmadh lá dég de mhí Iuil, is an m-bliadhain d'aeis an Tigherna 1857.*[7]

John Devoy was in no doubt that if the Fenians had been successful they would have undertaken the restoration of Irish: 'John O'Mahony would certainly have exercised great influence in that government'.[8] An earlier Young Ireland regime, where O'Mahony would be joined by Michael Doheny and Michael Cavanagh, would possess an Irish wing well capable of conserving as well as restoring that language.

Cavanagh who returned to Ireland in 1861 for the MacManus funeral, in his poem *Athchuairt go hÉireann* manages to capture both the transformation of Irish society and the émigré's lament for the land that was left behind.

> A! Níl aon ní mar a d'fhagas é
> Níl aon ní mar do bhí;

Níl feir ná magh chomh glás anois,
Níl fraoch ná gcnoc chomh buí.
In m'intinn níl na crainn chomh hárd,
Nó sléibhte leath chomh mór;
'S na sruthán, mheas mé in mo bhrón
Gur athruithe a nglór.

Och! Is athruithe na daoine féin
Nach trua é a gcás!
In a mbéala maireann teanga úr
Do fuair an Ghaelig bás
'Gus leithe d'eúg an spioraid thréin
Do chomhraigh in gach croí,
A, níl aon ní mar ba chóir é bheith,
Níl aon ní mar do bhí.

MICHAEL CAVANAGH

A Return Visit to Ireland

Oh, nothing as I left it there,
There's naught as it has been;
The heath has not so bright a bloom
The fields are not so green.
To me the trees seemed not so high,
The mountains so sublime;
Nor sang the rippling stream so sweet
As in my boyhood's time.

And worse than all, the men are changed
Oh, shame! that 'twould be said:
They only speak the tyrants' tongue
With them the Gaelic's dead:
And with it died the spirit bold
That e'er upheld the "Green"!
Ah nothing's as it was of old.
There's naught as it has been.[9]

For Cavanagh Irish remained the most modern of languages and in 1885
he managed to mark the death of Ulysses Simpson Grant Civil War hero
and two term President, with a fine yet simple poem. Grant was popular
among Irish Americans and regarded as a fellow Celt because of his
ancient Scots ancestry.

A gcuimhne ar U.S. Grant

Marbh! Inniu, faoi shíocht, faoi shuain,
Tá'n saighdiuir fíor!
Marbh! Tá'n laoch a sheas go buan
Ar son a thír!

A thír, do bhí le comhrac, fáin
O dheas go tuaidh;
O bhun go barr tá 'nois siocháin
Ba mhór an bhua!

Ciúin, cróga bhí sé inns an troid,
Le misneach lán,
Níor mhianaigh sé a bheith a mbroid
Fear dubh nó bán.

Níor, 'arr sé glóire ann aon bheart,
Ba mhór a chroí!
Ach tháinigh sí go cóir, go ceart
'gus las a shlí.

Ní fos ó chloinn a dhuthaighe féin
Do fuair sé modh,
Ach ann gach crích faoi sholus gréin
Bhí ónoir dhó.

Caoineamaois é, 'gus ní gan fáth,
Ór bhí a shaoil
'Na shampla fíor den'n bhri atá
A sliocht na nGaodhal.

Marbh! Ach béidh a chuimhne beo
'N ár measc go bráth;
Marbh! Ach béidh ar ngrá níos teo
Ag fás gach lá.

In Memoriam – U.S. Grant

Dead! To-day in peaceful rest
Lies the soldier grand!
Dead! The hero who raised his crest
For his native land!

His land, that, - weak through cruel strife,
From North to South,
Knew not that peace that now gives life,

His victory's worth.

Brave as his sword, in battle's need,
He only knew
His fellow man from bondage freed
What'er his hue.

He sought not fame: no glorious deed
His heart could sway;
But honour came, with well earned need
And lit his way.

Loved by the children of the soil,
From which he sprung,
In every land where freemen toil
His praise is sung.

We mourn him, mindful that his life
In naught did fail
To prove the worth, in sternest strife
Of the Clann-na-Gael.

Dead! But his memory shall glow
In our midst for aye!
Dead! But our love will warmer grow,
Day after day.[10]

Mention has already been made of Cavanagh's role in the establishment
and filling of the Celtic Chair in the Catholic University of Washington.
He was also very friendly with An Craoibhín Aoibhinn, a Roscommon
clergyman's son and helped to bring his work to the attention of Irish
American audiences.[11] Dubhglas de hÍde is better known as a founder of
Conradh na Gaeilge and first President of Ireland.

Today, it is only in Cappoquin that traces of 1849 still linger. If you go to
Old Affane cemetery, just outside the town; walk a few paces from the

WALSH'S HOTEL, CAPPOQUIN, 1998

gate and go in to your right and look for three tall gravestones and there you will find the Donohoes, James and John. Then go up to the ruined church and turn to the left and search for the headstone of sub-constable James Owens on which you will find inscribed 'murdered at Cappoquin'. Just behind him, in the family burial place, lies James Crotty. There are also four other stones, among the tangled vegetation, in the left-hand corner of the cemetery which mark the final resting places of five soldiers who died during the military occupation of Cappoquin. In the town the barracks is now Walsh's Hotel which stands in Allen Street which was re-named to commemorate that Manchester Martyr. The Mercy Nuns remained and their convent stands high up on the hill. In the 1960s a new terrace of houses was named after James Donohoe.

Finally it is interesting to speculate whether the long term impact of Young Ireland and 1849 was to entrench militant republicanism in certain parts of the South of Ireland. In the War of Independence, 70 years later,

I.R.A. units in South Tipperary, South Kilkenny and West Waterford were particularly active. The opposition to the Treaty was predominately Munster and Connacht based and it was Liam Lynch from the Galtee foothills like John O'Mahony, who almost single-handedly kept the Republicans in the field when all seemed lost. After his death in 1923 when shot on the Knockmealdown Mountains near Goatenbridge a much-depleted I.R.A. Army Executive, including representatives from Waterford and South Tipperary and Kilkenny, met at Poulacapple and decided to end all military operations.

KEANE'S GATE, CAPPOQUIN, 1998

Whatever the case it is hoped that this study has demonstrated that 1849 means much more that a small footnote in Bermuda's convict history or a few graves in Ireland, America and Tasmania. Rather it is vital towards appreciating the real significance and impact of the Young Ireland movement.

Notes:

1. See Breen, op. cit., pp. 26, 45-6; R. Kee, *The Most Distressful Country The Green Flag Vol 1*, London 1989, p. 291.

2. See Mitchel, op. cit., pp. 122, 124; Irish Citizen 1868; P. O'Shaughnessy ed., *The Gardens of Hell John Mitchel in Van Diemen's Land 1850-1853*, Kenthurst N.S.W., 1988 pp. 48, 51, 55-56, 79-80.

3. Ned Kelly, A Letter from Jerilderie, in B. Wannan ed., *The Wearing of the Green: The Lore, Literature, Legend and Balladry of the Irish in Australia*, Melbourne, 1965, p. 197. See also Amos, op. cit., and Kiely, The Connerys pp. 98-100.

4. Cavanagh,'Joseph Brenan', *Young Ireland*, 20 June 1885; Luby, Philip Gray, op. cit; Court Martial of Edmond Power, N.A., Rebellion Papers, 620/6/70/29; ibid Francis Hearn, 620/6/70/2; ibid., Philip Cunningham, 620/6/69/13; Cavanagh, 'To my kind old Neighbour Miss Mary O'Donnell on her nineteeth birthday May 1882', N.L.I., MS 3308, p. 153.

5. K.L. Maurice, op. cit.

6. See 'Herald of the Fenians A Forgotten Meathman', in *Wolfe Tone Annual* 1940, pp. 58-9.

7. J. O'Mahony ed., *Foras Feasa ar Eirinn*, New York, 1857, p. 739. The copy in N.L.I. ref. LO 4995 has annotations and appears to be O'Mahony's working copy.

8. J. Devoy, *Recollections of an Irish Rebel*, New York, 1929, p. 263.

9. Cavanagh, N.L.I., MS 3308, p. 271.

10. Ibid., p. 205.

11. See N.L.I., MS 3308.

12. E. Neeson, *The Civil War 1922-23*, 2nd ed., Dublin 1989, pp. 289-91; F. O'Donoghue, *No Other Law*, Dublin 1954.

Come To Me Dearest – Joseph Brenan

Come to me, dearest, I'm lonely without thee,
Day-time and night-time I'm thinking about thee;
Night-time and day-time in dreams I behold thee,
Unwelcome the waking which ceases to fold thee.
Come to me, darling, my sorrows to lighten,
Come in thy beauty to bless and to brighten,
Come in thy womanhood, meekly and lowly,
Come in thy lovingness queenly and holy.

Swallows will flit round the desolate ruin,
Telling of Spring and its joyous renewing;
And thoughts of thy love, and its manifold treasure,
Are circling my heart with a promise of pleasure;
O Spring of my spirit! O May of my bosom!
Shine out on my soul till it burgeon and blossom
The waste of my life has a rose root within it,
And thy fondness alone to the sunshine can win it.

Figure that moves like a song through the even
Features lit up by a reflex of heaven
Eyes like the skies of poor Erinn, our mother,
Where the shadows and sunshine are chasing each other;
Smiles coming seldom, but child-like and simple,
Planting in each rosy cheek a sweet dimple
Oh! Thanks to the Saviour that even thy seeming
Is left to the exile to brighten his dreaming!

You have been glad when you knew I was gladdened;
Dear, are you sad to hear I am saddened?
Our hearts ever answer in tune and in time, love,
As octave to octave and rhyme unto rhyme, love;

I cannot weep but your tears will be flowing
You cannot smile but my cheeks will be glowing
I would not die without you at my side, love
You will not linger when I shall have died, love.

Come to me, dear, ere I die of my sorrow,
Rise on my gloom like the sun of tomorrow,
Strong, swift and fond as the words which I speak, love,
With a song on your lip and a smile on your cheek, love.
Come, for my heart in your absence in weary
Haste for my spirit is sickened and dreary;
Come to the arms which alone should caress thee;
Come to the heart which is throbbing to press thee.

Brenan wrote this poem in New York for Mary Savage a few weeks
before their marriage there in 1851. Mary died in New York in 1862 and
of their seven children together only Florence survived infancy. She was
very talented like her father but decided to join the Sisters of Mercy. She
was based in Omaha, Nebraska at the turn of the nineteenth century.

Joseph Brenan - John Fitzgerald

He is resting afar from the land he ador'd;
But the soil of the brave is his pillow,
When he grasp'd not for Erin the conquering sword,
When he died far away o'er the billow;
For the coward deserted him, fearing the scars,
And the renegade sought to ensnare him,
Till he fled to the Land of the Banner of Stars,
Where the brave and the true would revere him.

He sung, while an exile, his dear native Lee,
Where he lovingly wandered in childhood,
And the glen where he dream'd he was happy and free,
As his rifle rang clear in the wild wood.

His warm young heart lov'd each mountain and sod,
And he fear'd neither hardship nor danger:
To rescue this land we were given by God
From the gripe of the cold-hearted stranger.

He died, though an exile, as free as the wind
The despot can reach him no longer;
There's a home for the slave where no tyrant can bind
And might over right is not stronger.
Then cherish his name in the home of his birth,
Though the traitor and slave may forget him;
While the heart beats responsive to virtue and worth
All the faithful and true shall regret him.

The above is from Fitzgerald's *Legends, Ballads and Songs of the Lee*, p. 26, published at Cork in 1862. It can also be sung to the air of Thomas Moore's *She is far from the Land*. Fitzgerald (1825-1910) who was known as the Bard of the Lee wrote, 'I have waited in vain for some one of more ability than myself to write something to our brave and talented young townsman. If my lines are far inferior to what he deserved, the fault is theirs not mine'.

Come back to Me - Mary Downing

My God! My Love! Come back to me,
My soul hath bitter need of Thee;
I cannot love, I cannot pray,
I cannot rest me night or day
In quiet thoughts of heaven and Thee:
My God! My Love! Come back to me.

Mysterious God! So far, so near,
Faith only tells me Thou are here;
As ever on Thy bounty fed,
As ever by Thy wisdom led,
Thy gifts have lost the look of Thee:
My God! My Love! Come back to me

Thy knowest 'tis but Thyself alone
Can fill the heart Thyself hast won;
If Thou shouldst give me leave to go
Back to the world, I could not now.
Poor and alone! I cry to Thee:
My God! My Love! Come back to me.

From *Voices from the Heart Sacred Poems* by Sr. Mary Alphonsus Downing, new and enlarged edition revised by Rt. Rev. Dr. Leahy Bishop of Dromore and published in Dublin in 1881. *Come back to Me* is on page 41.

Resurgam On raising the Green Flag on the Erin's Hope Easter Sunday 1867
Michael Cavanagh & John O'Mahony

May He who this day from the grave hath arisen,
In whose glory' the glad sun now dances on high,
Pour balm on the hearts of our brothers in prison,
And bless the green banner we fling to the sky!
Scaoiltear le gaoith gan moill an Gath Gréine
Thugamar féin an Samhradh linn
Agus seoltar ár long faoi bhratach na Féinne
Thugamar féin an Samhradh linn.

The flag of our sires, the old Sunburst of Tara,
Is rising to lighten our path o'er the wave,
Our isle 'twill illume from Benmore to Iveragh,
And gild with its harp the death bed of our brave.
Scaoiltear amach go luath an Gath Gréine,
Thugamar féin an Samhradh linn,
Agus triallamaois feasta faoi bhratach na Féinne
Thugamar féin an Samhradh linn.

Oh! See on the masthead, how gaily it dances!
Boys! Don't your hears leap at the soul thrilling sight?
St. Bride speed the day when o'er lines of red lances,
'Twill dash through the ranks of the foe in his flight.
Sin scaoilt os ár gceann go hárd an Gath Gréine,
Thugamar féin an Samhradh linn,
Agus raghmaois chun catha faoi bhratach na Féinne,
Thugamar féin an Samhradh linn.

Now fire a salute to its fame and God's glory,
Let guns and hosannas resound o'er the sea,
Twice blest be the day in our land's future story
That saw rise again the green flag of the Free.
Conguigidh slán go bráth an Gath Gréine
Thugamar féin an Samhradh linn;
Go ruaigfeann gach namhaid as bhailtibh na hÉireann,
Thugamar féin an Samhradh linn.

From N.L.I., MS 3308, pp. 101-3. See also MS 3307, p. 128 and J. Maher
ed, *Chief of the Comeraghs*, p. 26.

APPENDIX 2 CASUALTIES

The Widow McCormack's, Farrenrory, Ballingarry 29 July 1848

> Patrick McBride, farmer's boy, killed.
> Thomas Walsh, stonebreaker, killed.
> John Kavanagh, journalist, wounded.
> James Stephens, civil engineer, wounded.
> James Dwyer, aged 25, wounded.
> Michael Lyons, coalminer, aged 26 wounded.

Glenbower, 12 September 1848

> Patrick Keating, Rathclarish, farmer, killed.

Portlaw, 12 September 1848

> Mr. Wade, son of a stocking vendor from Kerry, killed.
> Michael Hart wounded.
> William Brennan wounded.

Rathgormack, 13 September 1848

> James Hahassy, Aughmore, farmer, wounded.

Cappoquin, 16 September 1849

> James Donohoe, aged 21, killed.
> James Owens, sub-constable, aged 26, died of wounds
> on 17th.

APPENDIX 3 CONVICTS

Brien, Richard: 5 6½, grey eyes, dark brown hair, fair complexion, small head, small visage, medium forehead, whiskers, crooked small finger on right hand, R.C., reads only; family 1850 wife Katherine, father Rodger and brother Michael.

Burke Thomas, 5 6, blue eyes, brown hair, fresh complexion, R.C., neither reads nor writes.

Callaghan, Martin: Native of Stradbally, Co. Wat., labourer, 5 3½, grey eyes, brown hair, fair complexion, R.C., neither reads nor writes, aged 20 in 1849, sentenced to 7 years transportation Co. Wat. Spring Assizes 1849 commuted to 2 years imprisonment. In Wat. Co. Gaol 26.1.1849 to 26.1.1851.

Casey, James: 5 1½, hazel eyes, brown hair, fair complexion, medium head, short visage, high forehead, double chin, scar on back of left arm, double chin, R.C., reads a little; family 1850 father James, brothers Philip & John, sisters Bridget & Katherine.

Crotty, James: 5 10½, grey eyes, dark brown hair, sallowy complexion with smallpox marks, R.C., neither reads nor writes.

Donohoe, John: 6 0, brown eyes, dark hair, fair complexion, R.C., reads & writes, went to national school.

Donovan, Thomas: 5 2½, grey eyes, dark hair, fresh complexion, medium head, oval visage, medium forehead, small scar over eyebrow, R.C., neither reads nor writes; family 1850 sister Mary.

Dowling, William Paul: 5 5½, brown eyes, light brown hair, fair complexion, medium head, oval visage, high forehead, whiskers, small mole on back of neck, R.C., reads & writes; family 1849 brothers John & Barth? sisters Ann & Margaret (America).

Doyle, William: 5 9, brown eyes, dark hair, fresh complexion, R.C., reads & writes.

Fay, Thomas: 5 3, brown eyes, dark brown hair, sallow complexion, oval visage, large head, low forehead, scars on chin, right face and bridge of nose, R.C., reads & writes: family 1849 father Patrick, brothers Charles & Patrick, sisters Maria & Elizabeth.

Joy, Mathew: 5 10½, grey eyes, dark hair, swarthy complexion, R.C., reads.

Keeffe, Cornelius: 5 5½, grey eyes, dark hair, swarthy complexion, large head, oval visage, low forehead, whiskers, squints, R.C., neither reads nor writes; family 1852 wife Johanna and brother Thomas.

Kenna, James: 5 4½, grey eyes, brown hair, fresh complexion, R.C., reads & writes, aged 56 in 1849 and sentenced to 10 years transportation Co. Wat. Summer Assizes 1849 but commuted to 18 months imprisonment. In Wat. Co.Gaol 5.2.1849 to 4.12.1850.

Kelly, William: 5 7½, blue eyes, brown hair, fresh complexion, R.C., neither reads nor writes.

Lennon, John: 5 8½, grey eyes, fair hair, fair complexion, R.C., reads & writes.

Lennon, Luke: 5 10, grey eyes, brown hair, fair complexion, R.C., reads & writes, went to national school.

Lynch, Bridget: 5 0½, grey eyes, black hair, fresh complexion, large head, oval visage, low forehead, large mouth and chin, R.C., neither reads nor writes, aged 19 in 1851. Family 1852 brothers Michael, Martin & Patrick.

Lyons, James: 6 1½, hazel eyes, brown hair, fresh complexion, medium head, large visage, broad forehead, whiskers, small moles on face, R.C., reads & writes; family 1850 mother Mary, brothers Michael & John, sisters Mary (America) and Statia.

Ryan, James: 5 6½, grey eyes, brown hair, fair complexion, R.C., reads & writes, aged 18 in 1849, sentenced to 14 years transportation Co. Wat. Summer Assizes 1850 commuted to 2 years imprisonment. In Wat. Co. Gaol 25.9.1849 to 25.9.1851.

Ryan, Thomas: 5 5, grey eyes, brown hair, fair complexion, R.C., reads & writes, aged 29 in 1849, sentenced to 14 years transportation Co. Wat. Summer Assizes 1850 commuted to 2 years imprisonment. In Wat. Co. Gaol 25.9.1849 to 25.9.1851

Shea, John: 5 5½, hazel eyes, dark brown hair, fresh complexion, oval head, medium visage and forehead, whiskers, pock marks on left arm, R.C., neither reads nor writes; family 1852 wife Mary? father Mathew? and brother Michael.

Sheafy, Edmond: 5 8½, grey eyes, brown hair, fair complexion, medium head, oval visage, high forehead, whiskers, scar left eyebrow, vaccinated right arm, R.C., reads & writes, went to private school; family 1851 wife Mary.

Tobin, Edward: 5 7, hazel eyes, dark hair, fresh complexion, narrow head & visage, high forehead, whiskers, scarred between eyebrows, R.C., neither reads nor writes; family 1850 wife Ellen, brother Michael, sisters Nancy, Mary & Katherine.

Wall, Thomas: 5 7½, blue eyes, brown hair, fresh complexion, medium head, oval visage, full forehead, whiskers, mole on upper lip, ring on ring finger left hand, R.C., reads & writes (reads a little in V.D.L. record); family 1850 father Michael, mother Catherine, brother James, sisters Ellen, Bridget, Mary & Nora.

Walsh, John: 5 10½, hazel eyes, dark brown hair, fresh complexion, long head, oval visage, full forehead, whiskers, scar on right cheek and cheek bone, ring on first and second finger of right hand, R.C., reads & writes; family 1850 mother Jane, brothers Andrew, James & Richard, sisters Nan & Ellen.

* Compiled using Clonmel, Galway County, Waterford County, Spike Island and Van Diemen's Land prison/convict records. Height is taken from Irish prison measurements. However, it should be noted that for some strange reason most lost a ½ inch on the voyage to Van Diemen's Land.

PRISONERS

Baker, Patrick: Sentenced 1 year Co. Wat. Summer Assizes 1849 for attacking Portlaw barracks and appearing in arms. In Wat. Co. Gaol 27.11.1848 to 27.11.1849.

Boshell, Martin: Clerk in counting house. Sentenced to 2 years at Liverpool Assizes on 11.12.1848 in Kirkdale Prison for conspiracy, aiding & assisting Irish in rebellion & to create insurrection, terror and alarm in England.

Brennan, John: Rathgormack district. Charged with appearing in arms & treasonable practices. In Wat. Co. Gaol from 21.9.1848 until bailed.

Brennan, John: Maryboro, Queen's Co., or Portlaw, labourer, aged 20, 5 9, grey eyes, brown hair, swarthy complexion, R.C., reads & writes. Sentenced 1 year Co. Wat. Summer Assizes 1849 from committal for attacking Portlaw barracks and appearing in arms. In Wat. Co. Gaol 22.9.1848 to 19.7.1849.

Brennan, William: Labourer, aged 15, 4 11, grey eyes, brown hair, fair complexion, R.C., reads. Acquitted at Co. Wat. Summer Assizes 1849 of attacking Portlaw Barracks. In Wat. Co. Gaol 19.9.1848 to 14.7.1849.

Bryan, John: Born in Boglanclea and lives in Ballingarry, labourer, aged 23, 5 8, fair hair, R.C., neither reads nor writes. Charged with being concerned in treasonable practices and attack on the police at Ballingarry. In Newgate Gaol 4.8.1848 to 11.11.1848 when discharged.

Butler, Thomas Jn: Aged 24, 5 5½, hazel eyes, fair hair, fresh complexion, R.C., neither reads nor writes, charged with attacking & burning Slate Quarries (Ahenny) barracks. In Clonmel Gaol 18.10.1848 to 19.3.1849.

Christopher, Michael: Clondaniel, Rathgormack & farmer? Charged with appearing in arms & treasonable practices. In Wat. Co. Gaol 21.9.1848 until bailed.

Cody, John: Carrickbeg, farmer, aged 53, 5 9½, grey eyes, brown hair, fresh complexion, R.C., reads & writes. Charged with being concerned in attack on Portlaw barracks but no bill at Co. Wat. Spring Assizes 1849. In Wat. Co. Gaol 2.10.1848 to 6.3.1849.

Collender, Hugh: Cappoquin, labourer, aged 20, 5 7½, grey eyes, brown hair, fair complexion, R.C., reads & writes. Convicted of trespass by P.C. Howley R.M., on 29.12.1848 and fined £5 or 1 month's imprisonment. In Wat. Co. Gaol 29.12.1848 to 29.1.1849.Where was he trespassing and what was he up to? John Lennon was caught with him and also served the same sentence.

Connell, Bryan: Mullinavat, Co. Kk., or Portlaw, labourer, aged 21, 5 11½, grey eyes, light hair, fresh complexion, R.C., reads. Sentenced to 1 year Co.Wat. Summer Assizes 1849 for attacking Portlaw barracks & appearing in arms. In Wat. Co. Gaol 29.11.1848 to 29.11.1849.

Connell, Timothy: Aged 29, 5 2, hazel eyes, black hair, fresh complexion, R.C., reads & writes. Charged with burning Slate Quarries barracks, appearing in arms and stealing and destroying the property of the constabulary. In Clonmel Gaol 20.9.1848 to 17.3.1849. Acquitted at Tipp. Spring Assizes 1849.

Comerford, Michael: Aged 27, 6 0½, grey eyes, brown hair, fresh complexion, R.C., neither reads nor writes. Details as Timothy Connell above.

Coonan, Patrick: Born Callan and lives in Ballingarry, farmer & shopkeeper, aged 35, 5 5, sandy hair, R.C., reads and writes. Charged with treasonable practices and attack on the police at Ballingarry. In Newgate Gaol 4.8.1848 to 1.9.1848 when removed to Richmond Bridewell.

Crotty, William: Aged 25, 5 5½, brown eyes, brown hair, fresh complexion, R.C., neither reads nor writes. Details as Timothy Connell

Cuddy, Joseph: gunshop salesman. See Martin Boshell above.

Dacres, Michael: Cappagh, Queens Co., labourer, aged 30, 5 7½, brown eyes, brown hair, fair complexion, R.C., neither reads nor writes. Sentenced to 1 year from committal at Co. Wat. Summer Assizes 1849 for attacking Portlaw barracks & appearing in arms. In Wat. Co. Gaol from 15.9.1848 to 15.9.1849.

Daly, Cornelius: Cappoquin, tailor, aged 24, 5 5½, grey eyes, dark hair, sallow complexion, R.C., reads & writes. Charged with murdering Sub-Constable Owens but no bill. In Wat. Co. Gaol 25.9.1849 to 8.5.1850.

Daniel, Andrew: Rathgormack district. Charged with appearing in arms & treasonable practices. In Wat. Co. Gaol 21.91848 until bailed.

Daniel, Richard: 5 10½, hazel eyes, dark brown hair, fresh complexion, R.C., reads & writes. Charged with burning Slate Quarries barracks, appearing in arms and stealing and destroying the property of the constabulary. In Clonmel Gaol 20.9.1848 to 17.3.1849. Acquitted at Tipp.

Spring Assizes 1849.

Davis, Richard: Blessington, Co. Wicklow, carman, aged 52, married, 5 0½, hazel eyes, brown hair, swarthy complexion, R.C., reads & writes. Sentenced to 6 months in Kilmainham Gaol from 27.7.1848 to 27.1.1849 for 'being found armed & arrayed in a warlike manner & traitorously assembled & gathered together with intent most maliciously to levy & make war against our sovereign majesty the Queen'.

Day, Patrick: Born in Lismolin and lives in Ballingarry, shoemaker, aged 31, 5 6, dark hair, R.C., reads. Charged with treasonable practices and attack on police at Ballingarry. In Newgate Gaol 4.8.1848 to 11.11.1848 when discharged.

Delamere, Peter, Herbert: Clerk in coal office. Acquitted at Liverpool Assizes on 21.12.1848 of conspiring to aid & assist Irish in rebellion & to create insurrection, terror and alarm in England.

Donovan, John: Portlaw, labourer, aged 23, 6 0, grey eyes, brown hair, fresh complexion, R.C., neither reads nor writes. Acquitted Co. Wat. Summer Assizes 1849 of engaging in insurrection. In Wat. Co. Gaol 22.9.1848 to 19.7.1849.

Doran, Fanton: Upper Wood, Queen's Co., cotton carder, aged 21, 5 11½, grey eyes, brown hair, fresh complexion, R.C., reads. Sentenced to 1 year from committal at Co. Wat. Summer Assizes 1849 for appearing in arms. In Wat. Co. Gaol 12.9.1848 to 12.9.1849

Doran, John: Born and lives in Boulea, Co. Tipp., labourer, aged 20, 5 7½, fair hair, R.C., reads and writes. Charged with treasonable practices and attack on police at Ballingarry. In Newgate Gaol 4.8.1848 to 11.11. 1848 when discharged.

Doran, Michael: Born and lives in Ballingarry, labourer, age 26, 5 7, light brown hair, R.C., neither reads nor writes. Details as John Doran above.

Dwyer, James: Aged 25, 5 6½, blue eyes, fair hair, fresh complexion, R.C., reads & writes. Committed to Clonmel Gaol on 17.8.1848 on charge of being one of a party who attacked the police on 29.7.1848 and was wounded. Discharged 14.11.1848 when bailed to Tipp. Spring Assizes 1849.

Dwyer, Michael: Born Limerick and lives in Ballingarry, coalminer, aged 28, 5 6, light brown hair, R.C., neither reads nor writes. Details as John Doran above.

Farrell, John: Born and lives in Ballingarry, storekeeper to outdoor relief, aged 20, fair hair, R.C., reads and writes. Details as John Doran above.

Finn, Thomas: Born Drangan lives in Ballingarry, carrier, aged 26, fair hair, R.C., reads and writes. Details as John Doran above.

Fitzpatrick, Richard: Cappoquin, labourer, aged 20, 5 6, blue eyes, brown hair, fair complexion, R.C., reads & writes. Charged with posting paper with pike or repeal on church gate. In Wat. Co. Gaol 14.8.1848 to 12.3.1849.

Flanagan, Michael: Acquitted at Co. Wat. Summer Assizes 1849 of drilling insurgents. In Wat. Co. Gaol 9.10.1848 to 19.7.1849.

Fleming, Walter: Portlaw, blacksmith, aged 30, 5 7½, grey eyes, dark hair, dark complexion, R.C., reads & writes. Charged with making pikes but no bill at Co. Wat. Spring Assizes. In Wat Co. Gaol 16.10.1848 to 6.3.1849.

Foley, John: Portlaw: labourer, 5 7½, blue eyes, dark brown hair, fresh complexion, R.C., neither reads nor writes. Sentenced to 1 year Co. Wat. Spring Assizes 1849 for appearing in arms & attacking Portlaw barracks. In Wat. Co. Gaol 19.9.1848 to 19.9.1849.

Foley, Michael: Acquitted at Co Wat. Spring Assizes 1849 of appearing in arms & being part of an insurrectionary movement. In Wat. Co. Gaol 21.9.1848 to 6.3.1849.

Gray, John: Coles Lane, Dublin, butcher, aged 25, 5 6, grey eyes, brown hair, fresh complexion, R.C., reads & writes. Charged on 29.7.1848 with having ball, cartridge & powder in his possession. Sentenced in Dublin on 21.10.1848 to 6 months from 27.7.1848 for unlawful conspiracy & traitorously levying war against her Majesty & to give bail to keep the peace for 7 years. In Kilmainham Gaol to 27.1.1849.

Griffin, Thomas: Carrigina near Carrick-on-Suir, horse breaker, aged 28, 5 2½, grey eyes, dark hair, fresh complexion, R.C., neither reads nor writes. Sentenced to 2 years at Co. Wat. Spring Assizes 1849 for appearing in arms etc. at Rathgormack. In Wat. Co. Gaol 26.9.1848 to 6.3.1851.

Hannegan, Patrick: Amber Hill near the Sweep, Kilmeaden, Co. Wat., labourer, aged 28, 5 10, grey eyes, dark hair, dark complexion, R.C., neither reads nor writes. Sentenced 1 year Co. Wat. Summer Assizes 1849 for appearing in arms & attacking Portlaw barracks. In Wat. Co. Gaol 23.9.1848 to 23.9.1849.

Hayes, John: Aged 18, 5 10½, grey eyes, brown hair, fresh complexion, R.C., reads & writes. Charged with burning Slate Quarries barracks, appearing in arms and stealing and destroying the property of the constabulary. In Clonmel Gaol 20.9.1848 to 17.3.1849. Acquitted at Tipp. Spring Assizes 1849.

Hearne, James: Ballythomas, Co. Wat., labourer, aged 27, 5 5½, grey eyes, brown hair, fresh complexion, R.C., neither reads nor writes. Charged with appearing in arms & being guilty of treasonable practices at Rathgormack. In Wat. Co. Gaol 21.9.1848 until bailed.

Hewson, Joseph: Portlaw, labourer, 5 8½, grey eyes, brown hair, fresh complexion. Sentenced to 2 years from committal at Co. Wat. Summer

Assizes 1849 for appearing in arms & attacking Portlaw barracks. In Wat. Co. Gaol 12.9.1848 to 12.9.1850.

Hickey, James: Aged 40, 5 7, brown eyes, brown hair, fresh complexion, R.C., neither reads nor writes. Charged with attacking & burning Slate Quarries barracks. In Clonmel Gaol 5.1.1849 to 19.3.1849.

Holihan, John: Park, Co. Wat., farmer, charged with appearing in arms & treasonable practices. In Wat. Co. Gaol 21.9.1848 until bailed.

Holihan, Murtagh: Scartlea, Co.Wat., farmer, charged with appearing in arms & treasonable practices. In Wat. Co. Gaol 21.9.1848 until bailed on 4.11.1848.

Hopper, Robert: Joiner at Birkenhead. Sentenced to 2 years at Liverpool Assizes on 11.12.1848 in Lancaster Castle for conspiracy to aid & assist the Irish in rebellion & to create insurrection, terror & alarm in England.

Hunt, William: Acquitted at Co. Wat. Summer Assizes 1849 of attacking Portlaw barracks. In Wat. Co. Gaol 29.11.1848 to 14.9.1849.

Joy, Michael: Killowen, Portlaw, farmer, aged 30, 5 9½, blue eyes, sandy hair, R.C., reads & writes. Acquitted at Co Wat. Summer Assizes 1849 of being engaged in Portlaw insurrection. In Wat. Co. Gaol 22.9.1848 to 19.7.1849.

Keating, John: Born and lives in Ballingarry, shoemaker, aged 30, 5 6, brown hair, R.C. reads and writes. Details as John Doran above.

Kelly, William: Sentenced to 2 years at Co. Wat. Spring Assizes 1849 for appearing in arms. In Wat. Co. Gaol 6.10.1848 to 6.3.1851.

Killilea, John: Owner & editor of *Waterford Chronicle*, aged 29, 6 0, hazel eyes, light brown hair, fresh complexion. Charged with treasonable practices & aiding, assisting & succouring John O' Mahony. In Clonmel Gaol 27.9.1848 to 10.2.1849.

Landers, Pierce: Rathdowney, Queen's Co., labourer, aged 62, 5 2½, grey eyes, grey hair, fresh complexion, R.C., reads & writes. Sentenced to 1 year from committal at Co. Wat. Summer Assizes 1849 for attacking Portlaw barracks & appearing in arms.

Landregan, Edmond: Aged 34, 5 6, hazel eyes, dark brown hair, fresh complexion, R.C., neither reads nor writes. Charged with burning the Slate Quarries barracks, appearing in arms and stealing and destroying the property of the constabulary. In Clonmel Gaol 20.9.1848 to 17.3.1849. Acquitted at Tipp. Spring Assizes 1849.

Landregan, James: Aged 48, 5 7½, hazel eyes, grey hair, fresh complexion, R.C., reads & writes. Charged with attacking Slate Quarries barracks and stealing and destroying the property of the constabulary. In Clonmel Gaol 20.9.1848 to 17.3.1849. Acquitted at Tipp. Spring Assizes 1849.

Lonergan, James: Aged 21, 5 8, grey eyes, brown hair, fresh complexion, R.C., reads & writes. Charged with attacking Slate Quarries & Portlaw barracks. In Clonmel Gaol 5.2.1849 to 19.3.1849.

Lyne or Tyne, Denis: Born and lives in Kilbrough, Co. Tipp., farmer, aged 25, 5 9, light brown hair, R.C., reads. In Newgate Gaol 4.8.1848 to 18.9.1848 when transferred to Clonmel under the Lord Lieutenant's warrant.

Lyons, Michael: Born and lives in Ballingarry, coalminer, aged 26, 5 7, brown hair, wounded in the shoulder, R.C., neither reads nor writes. Charged with treasonable practices and attack on police at Ballingarry. In Newgate Gaol 4.8.1848 to 11.12.1848 when sent to Dublin Metropolitan police office.

Lyons otherwise Fahey otherwise Reilly, Bridget: Aged 34, 4th committal since 1845. Acquitted at Co Wat. Summer Assizes 1850 of being armed & attacking Cappoquin barracks. In Wat. Co. Gaol 29.9.1849 to 13.7.1850.

Lyons, John: Curraghkiely, Rathgormack, carpenter, aged 33, 5 7½, grey eyes, brown hair, fresh complexion, R.C. neither reads nor writes. Charged with appearing in arms & treasonable practices. In Wat. Co. Gaol 21.9.1848 until bailed.

McCarthy, Daniel: Brunswick St., Cork, baker, aged 25, 5 5, grey eyes, brown hair, fair complexion, R.C., reads & writes. Sentenced to 1 year from committal at Co. Wat. Summer Assizes 1849 for appearing in arms. In Clonmel Gaol 1.10.1848 to 3.1.1849, in Wat. Co. Gaol 6.1.1849 to 6.1.1850.

Maher, Edmond: Born and lives in Ballingarry, shoemaker, aged 22, light brown hair, R.C., reads and writes. Details as John Doran above.

Maher, James: Born Gortnahue and lives in Ballingarry, cooper, aged 45, 5 5, dark hair, R.C., reads and writes. Details as John Doran above.

Maher, Thomas: Rathgormack, publican. Acquitted at Co. Wat. Spring Assizes 1849 of appearing in arms & being part of an insurrectionary movement at Rathgormack. In Wat. Co. Gaol 21.9.1848 to 6.3.1849.

Malone, James: Kilmacow, Co. Kk., labourer, aged 29. Sentenced to 2 years at Kk. Spring Assizes for attacking Kilmacow barracks. Had a wife and two young children and no previous convictions. In Kk. Gaol from 19.9.48 to 19.9.1850? See C.R.F. M36/1850.

Moore, John: Aged 19, 5 11, grey eyes, brown hair, sallow complexion, R.C., reads & writes. Charged with burning the Slate Quarries barracks, appearing in arms and stealing and destroying the property of the constabulary. In Clonmel Gaol 20.9.1849 to 17.3.1849. Acquitted at Tipp. Spring Assizes 1849.

Morrissey, Patrick: Filer & Fitter, aged 20, 5 0, brown eyes, dark hair, swarthy complexion, R.C., neither reads nor writes. Acquitted at Co. Wat. Spring Assizes 1849 of attacking Portlaw barracks. In Wat. Co. Gaol 10.10.1848 to 9.3.1849.

Mulcahy, James: Rathgormack Dist., charged with appearing in arms & treasonable practices. In Wat. Co. Gaol 21.9.1848 until bailed.

Mulcahy, Michael: Curraghballintlea near Portlaw, labourer, aged 25, 5 10, grey eyes brown hair, fresh complexion, R.C., reads. Sentenced to 2 years from committal at Co. Wat. Spring Assizes 1849 for appearing in arms at Portlaw. In Wat Co. Gaol 13.10.1848 to 13.10.1850.

Mulcahy, William: Rathgormack district. Charged with appearing in arms & treasonable practices. In Wat. Co. Gaol 21.9.1848 until bailed.

Murphy, Edward: Secretary of the Liverpool Sarsfield Club, a doctor? He was arrested on 17.8.1848 – pikeheads found in his house and charged with conspiracy. He appears to have been convicted at the Liverpool Assizes on 11.12.1848 but the *Times'* account, in list of sentences, mention a Murphy getting 3 months in Kirkdale account being taken of time already served. Did himself and Patrick Murphy below get the same sentence?

Murphy, Maurice: Clonmel, shoemaker, aged 22, 5 1½, blue eyes, auburn hair, fresh complexion, R.C., reads & writes. Arrested at Sir Thomas Osborne's Bridge, Kilsheelan with pike under coat & supply of bread, meat & whiskey. Sentenced to 2 years hard labour at Clonmel October Quarter Session 1848. In Clonmel Gaol 12.9.1848 to 28.6.1849 when discharged by order of the Lord Lieutenant. See *Waterford Mail*, 18 September and *Tipperary Free Press*, 23 October 1848.

Murphy, Patrick: A Liverpool tailor. See Edward Murphy above.

Neill, James: Aged 40, 5 8½, grey eyes, brown hair, fresh complexion, R.C., neither reads nor writes. Charged with burning the Slate Quarries barracks, appearing in arms & stealing & destroying the property of the constabulary. In Clomel Gaol 20.9.1848 to 17.3.1849. Acquitted at Tipp. Spring Assizes 1849.

O'Brien, James: Labourer in Liverpool. Sentenced to 6 months at

Liverpool Assizes on 11.12.1848 for conspiracy to aid & assist Irish in rebellion & create insurrection, terror and alarm in England. Imprisoned in Lancaster Castle.

O'Donnell, Francis: Surgeon. Sentenced to 2 years at Liverpool Assizes on 11.12.1848 on same charges as James O'Brien. Imprisoned in Lancaster Castle.

Orchard or Archer, James: Born and lives in Killenaule, Co. Tipp., labourer, aged 35, 5 7, brown hair, R.C., reads. Details as Denis Lyne above.

Owens, Michael: Three Bridges (on road from Carrick to Piltown) or Portlaw, gaiter or factory overseer, aged 27, 5 1, hazel eyes, dark hair, swarthy complexion, R.C., neither reads nor writes. Sentenced to 1 year from committal at Co. Wat. Summer Assizes 1849 for attack on Portlaw barracks. In Wat. Co. Gaol 16.10.1848 to 16.10.1849?

Quirke, William: Clonmel, cutler, aged 29, 5 4, grey eyes, black hair, fresh complexion, R.C., reads & writes. Details as Maurice Murphy.

Power, Catherine: Ring, Co. Wat., labourer, aged 42, 5 2½, grey eyes, brown hair, fresh complexion, R.C., neither reads nor writes. Acquitted at Co. Wat. Summer Assizes 1850 of being armed & attacking Cappoquin barracks. In Wat. Co. Gaol 29.9.1849 to 13.7.1850.

Power, Ellen Mary: Aged 25, 5 4½, hazel eyes, brown hair, fresh complexion, R.C., reads & writes. Charged with having gunpowder, balls & shot in a proclaimed district & aiding etc. John O'Mahony. In Clonmel Gaol 27.9.1848 to 4.10.1849.

Power, Michael: Acquitted at Co. Wat. Summer Assizes 1849 of attacking Portlaw barracks. In Wat. Co. Gaol 27.11.1848 to 14.7.1849.

Rochford, William: Aged 40, 5 5½, blue eyes, brown hair, fresh complexion, R.C., neither reads nor writes. Charged with burning Slate

Quarries barracks, appearing in arms and stealing and destroying the property of the constabulary. In Clonmel Gaol 20.9.1848 to 17.3.1849. Acquitted at Tipp. Spring Assizes 1849.

Shea, John: Born and lives in Ballingarry, carpenter, aged 19, 5 6, fair hair, R.C., reads and writes. Details as John Doran above.

Sheedy, James: Aged 28, 5 8, hazel eyes, black hair, fresh complexion, R.C., reads & writes. Charged with burning Slate Quarries barracks, appearing in arms and stealing and destroying the property of the constabulary. In Clonmel Gaol 20.9.1848 to 17.3.1849. Acquitted at Tipp. Spring Assizes 1849.

Sheehan, John, V: Dungarvan Co. Wat., draper, aged 21, 5 3½, grey eyes, sandy hair, fair complexion. He was working in Dublin when arrested and charged with treasonable practices. In Kilmainham Gaol 31.7.1848 to 23.9.1848 when bailed. He later went to America where he married. He died of a brain tumour in Newark New Jersey on 2.4.1856. His father William was a prominent Dungarvan merchant. See *Waterford News,* 9 May 1856

Slyney, Edmond: Ballintaylor, Co Wat., labourer, aged 33, 5 5½, grey eyes, dark hair, fair complexion, R.C. Sentenced to 1 year from committal at Co. Wat. Summer Assizes 1849 for appearing in arms. In Wat. Co. Gaol 5.1.1849 to 5.1.1850. Edward Slaney in newspaper report.

Smith, Michael: Born and lives in Kilcooley, Co. Tipp., coalminer, aged 23, 5 4, brown hair, R.C., reads. Charged with treasonable practices and attack on police at Ballingarry. In Newgate Gaol 4 .8.1848 to 10.1.1849 when returned to Tipperary.

Smyth, George: Hatter in Liverpool. Sentenced to 2 years at Liverpool Assizes on 11.12.1848 for conspiracy to aid & assist the Irish in rebellion and create insurrection, terror & alarm in England. Imprisoned in Lancaster Castle.

Somers, Mathew: Details as George Smyth above.

Stack, Thomas: Born and lives in Ballingarry, labourer, aged 30, 6 1, fair hair, R.C., neither reads nor writes. Details as Denis Lyne above.

Stone, Thomas: Freshford, Co. Kk., labourer, aged 22, 6 0½, grey eyes, sandy hair, fresh complexion, Prot., reads & writes. Acquitted Co. Wat. Summer Assizes 1849 of attacking Portlaw barracks & appearing in arms. In Wat. Co. Gaol 19.9.1848 to 18.7.1849.

Sullivan, Denis Jn: Monadiha, Mothel, farmer, aged 30, 5 9½, hazel eyes, dark hair, fresh complexion, R.C., neither reads nor writes. Charged with appearing in arms & treasonable practices at Rathgormack. In Wat. Co. Gaol 21.9.1848 to 11.1.1849 when bailed.

Sullivan, Denis Sn: Ballythomas, Mothel, labourer, aged 35, grey eyes, brown hair, fresh complexion, R.C., neither reads nor writes. Charged with appearing in arms & treasonable practices. In Wat. Co. Gaol 21.9.1848 until bailed.

Sullivan, Jeremiah: Sentenced to 1 year from committal at Co. Wat. Summer Assizes 1849 for appearing in arms & attacking Portlaw barracks. In Wat . Co. Gaol 19.9.1848 to 19.9.1849.

Sullivan, John: Born in Kyle and lives in Boulea, Co. Tipp., farmer, aged 34, brown hair, R.C., neither reads nor writes. Details as John Doran above.

Sullivan, John: Kenmare, Co. Ky., tailor, aged 24, 5 2½, grey eyes, dark hair, swarthy complexion, R.C., reads & writes. Acquitted at Co. Wat. Summer Assizes 1849 of attacking Portlaw barracks. In Wat. Co. Gaol 14.9.1848 to 19.7.1849.

Toner, Thomas: Born Dover, England lives in Ballingarry, coalminer, aged 33, 6 0, brown hair, R.C., reads. Charged with treasonable practices and attack on the police at Ballingarry. In Newgate Gaol 4.8.1848 to

25.11.1848 when sent to Dublin Metropolitan police office.

Tunny, Nicholas: Rathgormack, blacksmith, aged 16, 5 7½, brown eyes, brown hair, swarthy complexion, R.C. Charged with appearing in arms & being guilty of treasonable practices. In Wat. Co. Gaol 21.9.1848 to 11.1.1849 when bailed to next assizes.

Walsh, John: Portlaw, fitter & filer of machinery, aged 25, 5 9½, hazel eyes, dark hair, fair complexion, R.C., reads & writes. Sentenced to 1 year from committal at Co. Wat. Summer Assizes 1849 of attacking Portlaw barracks & appearing in arms. In Wat. Co. Gaol 15.9.1849 to 15.9.1850.

Walsh, Patrick: Aged 17, 5 4, hazel eyes, brown hair, fresh complexion, R.C, reads & writes. Charged with burning the Slate Quarries barracks, appearing in arms & destroying & stealing the property of the constabulary. In Clonmel Gaol 20.9.1848 to 17.3.1849. Acquitted at Tipp. Spring Assizes 1849.

Whelan or Phelan, James: Born and lives in Ballingarry, carrier, aged 20, 5 8, brown hair, R.C., neither reads nor writes. Charged with treasonable practices and attack on the police at Ballingarry. In Newgate Gaol 4.8.1848 to 11.11.1848 when discharged.

* Compiled using Clonmel, Kilmainham, Newgate and Waterford County prison records. For the Liverpool prisoners see Chapter 3, no. 85. See also other references where given.

APPENDIX 4
HEROES, INFORMERS & CONCERNED CITIZENS

The constabulary who defended Cappoquin barracks received rewards similar to their comrades at Portlaw the year before. They were presented with badges of merit and sub-constable Olden who was the most senior, was promoted to constable. Poor James Owen's father was awarded 100 guineas from the Waterford Grand Jury.[1]

After the Summer Assizes of 1850 the Informers John Brien and James Connell were brought to Dublin and given government passages for New York. John Yorick felt New York was more dangerous than Cappoquin so he remained behind and was allowed to keep his £22.[2] However, on the night of 7 May 1851 the carriage of Leopold Keane, son of Sir Richard Keane, and his wife was fired on as it returned to town from a dinner party in Richmond House. The gunman was never caught but George Hill in a subtle letter to Sir Thomas Redington, the Under Secretary, pointed the finger at Yorick. Yorick it seems was already facing charges for firing a shot at a young man, the son of a nailer and had spent time in custody for threatening 'a young man of the name of Lennon'.[3] It seems a bit more than a coincidence but in August Yorick addressed a memorial to Clarendon saying he was now anxious to leave the service of Sir Richard Keane and wished to be sent to Halifax, Nova Scotia. He had been a constable in 1835 in Leinster under Inspector General John Harvey who was now Governor of Nova Scotia so he was optimistic of employment prospects there. Yorick claimed to have since March 1850 'been persecuted and annoyed by the evil-disposed inhabitants of Cappoquin'.[4]

However, the government was only willing to send him to Quebec or New York so Yorick had little choice for in the latter 'I would have a better chance of preserving my life here. The leaders of the late Cappoquin Insurrection being there'.[5] He also felt Quebec was too cold for his wife Julia and infant John. However, Quebec it had to be and Yorick and his family sailed from Waterford on the *Lady Campbell* on 12 September 1851.[6] Needless to say, arriving just in time for the harsh

Canadian Winter, Yorick found the going tough. On 13 January 1852 he wrote to his contact P.C. Howley R.M., asking him to use his influence with the Irish government to get him some kind of job as 'I don't know what I'll do when the money which the Government gave me is expended'.[7] Howley raised his case with government but to no avail. The Under Secretary Redington put it bluntly; 'His Excellency considers John Yorick to have been fully remunerated & to have no further claim upon the consideration of the Government. His Excellency has no control over Colonial appointments'.[8] There is no more correspondence on the file so presumably Yorick had to fend for himself.

Another ex-policeman Patrick Masterson O'Rourke caused a flurry of excitement when he wrote to the County Waterford police in April 1850 claiming that two of his comrades, Michael Hurley and Timothy Morrissey, in the East India Company service, at Brentwood, Essex had been present at the wounding of James Owens. O'Rourke had been dismissed from the County Cork constabulary and, according to Henry J. Brownrigg, Deputy Inspector of the Irish Constabulary, was 'a man of very bad character – it is not unreasonable to suppose that the whole thing may have been concocted by Rourke & the others – for the purpose of being brought back to this country'.[9] However, he gave permission to the County Waterford police to proceed on the matter and warrants were issued for the arrest of Hurley and Morrissey. At the same time in Cappoquin it was rumoured that Hurley was about to become an informer. It is unclear what happened when the police went to Essex for it has not been possible to locate a file which contains a letter dated 10 May 1850 from County Inspector John Clarke on the case.[10] However, it seems likely that nothing came of it as it surely would have had a major impact on the County Waterford Summer Assizes of 1850.

Notes:

1. *Waterford News,* 19 October 1849, *Waterford Mail,* 20 October 1849, Breen, op. cit., p. 70.
2. Memorial of J. Yorick, 2 September 1850, N.A., O.P., 29/206/1850.
3. G. Hill to Redington, 13 May 1851, ibid, 29/150/1851.

4. Memorial of J. Yorick August 1851; ibid, 29/28/1852.
5. J. Yorick, 20 August 1851, ibid.
6. *Waterford Mail,* 13 September 1851.
7. Yorick to Howley, 13 January 1852, N.A., O.P., 29/28/1852.
8. Redington to Howley, 21 February 1852, ibid.
9. H.R. Brownrigg, 30 April 1850, N.A., O.P., 29/118/1850.
10. Ref. to file 29/126/1850 in N.A., Index to Registered Papers 1850, 1 Division, Vol. 2.

APPENDIX 5 EMIGRANT GIRLS

Carthy, Mary: Born Tallow, Co. Cork, house servant, aged 20, R.C., in good health, parents John & Elizabeth living in Cappoquin, no relations in New South Wales.

Cunnigham, Mary: Born Cappoquin, farm servant, aged 20, parents Daniel and Margaret living in Cappoquin.

Dwyer, Ann: Born Cappoquin, nursemaid, aged 21, R.C., neither reads nor writes, parents Edmund and Mary living in Cappoquin, uncle William Dwyer in New South Wales.

Griffin, Mary: Born Cappoquin, nursemaid, aged 16, R.C., parents Patrick and Johanna living in Cappoquin, no relatives in New South Wales.

Keeffe, Mary: Born Cappoquin, farm servant, aged 19, R.C., neither reads nor writes, parents John and Margaret living in Cappoquin, no relatives in New South Wales.

Kennedy, Mary: Born Halifax, Nova Scotia, house servant, aged 25, Church of England, reads & writes, parents Thomas and Ellen living in Cappoquin, sisters Caroline and Ann Kennedy in New South Wales.

Linnen, Mary: Born Cappoquin, house servant, aged 19, R.C., neither reads nor writes, parents John and Catherine living in Cappoquin.

Trehey, Jane: Born Cappoquin, house servant, aged 21, R.C., reads & writes, in good health, parents John and Mary living in Cappoquin, no relatives in New South Wales.

Wall, Bridget: Born Cappoquin, house servant, aged 19, R.C., neither reads nor writes, in good health, parents Michael and Catherine in Cappoquin, no relatives in New South Wales.

Wall, Mary: Born Cappoquin, house servant, aged 21, R.C., neither reads nor writes, in good health, parents James and Ann living in Cappoquin, no relatives in New South Wales.

Walsh, Bridget: House servant, aged 19, R.C., neither reads nor writes, parents James and Ellen living in Cappoquin, no relatives in New South Wales.

Welstead, Margaret: Born Cappoquin, house servant, aged 23, neither reads nor writes, in good health, parents Thomas and Mary dead, no relatives in New South Wales.

The ship *Success* left Plymouth, England on 1 August 1849 with some families of convicts and 182 government emigrants. She arrived in Hobart, Tasmania on 21 November and is listed as having 218 emigrants and five cabin passengers on board. She left Hobart on 9 December and deposited her passengers in Sydney on 17 December 1849. See *Hobart Courier,* 24 November and 12 December 1849 and *Sydney Morning Herald,* 19 December 1849. See also List of *Success* Immigrants as inspected by the Immigration Board on 18 December 1849 in A.O.N.S.W. 4/4914 & 50/130 in 9/6194.

BIBLIOGRAPHY

1. Manuscripts

Archives Office of New South Wales
Assisted Emigrants *Success* 1849 MSS 4/4914, 50/130 in 9/6194.

Archives Office of Tasmania
C.B. 7/15/1 & 16/1.
Con. 2/364; 14/32, 38, 42-3; 15/8; 33/100, 104, 109, 112; 41/36; 52/7;
56/3 & 76/1.
C.S.O. 24/252/10266.
L.C. 282/1.
L.S.D. 1/80.
Misc. Photographs 31/239 (Catherine Bennett).
M.B. 2/39/18.
S.C. 195/36.
Wayne Index.

Catholic University of America, Washington D.C.
Fenian Brotherhood Records 1855-1910. Boxes 1-4.

Cornelian Bay Cemetery, Hobart
Burial Register 1898.

Library of Tasmania
J.H. Cullen MS.

Mitchell Library, Sydney
Journal of C.A. Anderson & *Lord Dalhousie* papers, in Returns from Irish
Convict Ships MS FM 4/3/32.

National Archives of Ireland
C.S.O. Government Com. Book 2 January 1849 to 29 December 1851;
Index to Registered Papers 1850, 1 Division, vol. 2.
C.R.F. Index 1849, C62/1849; D41, K3, L26, M36, R28/1850; B8/1851.

G.P.O., CN6, Spike Island, 624, 656-7/1855, 25, 97, 112/1856.
O.P., 29/138, 370, 380, 411, 415/1849; 29/118, 206, 263/1850; 29/150/1851; 29/28, 177, 221/1852.
Prisons. Clonmel 1/7/4; Galway County 1/21/3-4; Kilmainham 1/10/8; Newgate 1/12/2; Waterford County 1/39/2-4.
Wills Ireland 1860.

National Library of Ireland
Michael Cavanagh MSS 3307-9.
Thomas Clarke Luby MSS 331-3.
Fenian Album MS 5957.
Spike Island Convict Register MS 3016.

National Museum of Ireland
Battle of Ridgeway, C.W. Desperate Charge of the Fenians under Col. O'Neill near Ridgeway Station June 2 1866, Print, Buffalo, New York 1869.

Public Records Office, London
Colonial Office, Bermuda, C.O., 37/127-8, 136, 138, 141, 144, 146-8 & 151.
Home Office, Hulk Registers, H.O., 8/102-20, 123 & 126.
Journal of J.W. Elliot, Adm., 101/13/4.
Journal of T. Keown, Adm., 101/59/3.

Saint Mary's Church, Cappoquin
Marriages Register 1849.

2. Newpapers

Bermuda Herald, 1854.
Citizen, New York, 1849.
Colonial Times and Tasmanian, 1854.
Cork Examiner, 1848-9, 1854-7, 1860, 1869.
Daily Picayune, New Orleans, 1857.
Derwent Valley Gazette, New Norfolk, 1996.

Dublin Evening Post, 1856.
Evening Echo, Cork, 1966.
Freeman's Journal, Dublin, 1854.
Hobart Town Courier, 1854.
Hobart Town Gazette, 1849, 1852-5, 1883, 1885.
Illustrated London News, 1848.
Independent on Sunday, London, 1998.
Irish Citizen, New York, 1868.
Irish Exile and Freedom's Advocate, Hobart, 1850.
Irishman, Dublin, 1849.
Irish Nation, New York, 1882.
Irish News, New York, 1857.
Irish People, Dublin, 1863-5.
Irish World, New York, 1877.
Limerick Reporter, 1847.
Mercury, Hobart, 1852, 1883, 1894, 1938.
Munster Advertiser, Carrick & Dungarvan, 1852.
New Orleans Delta, 1852.
New York Sun.
Observer, London, 1856.
Tipperary Free Press, Clonmel, 1849.
Times, London, 1848.
Tribune, Dublin, 1855-6.
Sunday Tribune, Dublin, 1998.
Sydney Morning Herald, 1849.
Waterford Chronicle, 1848.
Waterford Mail, 1848-51.
Waterford News, 1849, 1852 & 1856.

3. Publications

Angus, M., Mather, F., Phillips, A., Smith, P.A. & Woodberry. J., *Historic Tasmania Sketchbook* (Maryborough Vic., 1977).
Amos, K., *The Fenians in Australia 1865-1880* (Kensington N.S.W., 1988).

Arthure, R., *A Priest of His Times Patrick Fogarty (1791-1866)*(Midleton, 1998).

Australian Dictionary of Biography, vol 1 (Melbourne, 1966).

Baker, A.D., *The Life and Times of Sir Richard Dry Eminent Tasmanian Statesman* (Hobart, 1951).

Barnet, J., & Brucker, A., *Central Criminal Court Session Papers,* vol XXVIII (London, 1848).

Bateson, C., *The Convict Ships 1878-1868* (Glasgow, 1985).

Battersby's Catholic Directory (Dublin 1848-57).

Bolger, P., *Hobart Town* (Canberra, 1973).

Bourke, M., *John O' Leary A Study in Irish Seperatism* (Tralee, 1967).

Boylan, H. ed., *A Dictionary of Irish Biography,* 3rd ed., (Dublin, 1998).

Brand, I., *The Convict Probation System: Van Diemen's Land 1839-1854* (Hobart, 1990).

Breathnach, D., & Ní Mhurchú, M., *1882-1992: Beathaisnéis A hAon* (Baile Átha Cliath, 1986).

_____, *1882-1992: Beathaisnéis A Dó* (Baile Átha Cliath, 1990).

Breathnach, E., *History Lore & Legend through the eyes of the Young* (Waterford, 1987).

Breathnach, N., Ar Bóthar Dom (An Rinn, 1998).

Brenan, J., *The Only Road* (Dublin, 1849).

Buckley, J.N., *James Fintan Lalor: Radical* (Cork, 1990).

Camn, J.C., & McQuiston, J., *Australians: A Historical Atlas* (Sydney, 1987).

Case, H.J., & Cooper, S.W., *Town of Darien 1641-1935* (Darien Conn., 1935).

Cavanagh, M., 'Joseph Brenan', *Young Ireland* 1885.

_____, *Memoirs of Gen. Thomas Francis Meagher* (Worcester Mass., 1892).

_____, *Waterford Celebreties* (Waterford, 1900).

Clarke, C.M.H., *The Earth Aludeth for Ever 1851-1888 A History of Australia,* vol IV (Melbourne, 1980).

Cocker, M., 'The Last Tasmanian', *Independent on Sunday* (26 April 1998) mag. pp. 10-13.

Comerford, R.V., *The Fenians in Context Irish Politics & Society 1848-*

82 (Dublin, 1985).

Condon, K., *The Missionary College of All Hallows 1842-1891* (Dublin, 1986).

Conlon, J.F., 'Mary of the Nation', *Evening Echo* (21 January 1966).

_____, *Some Irish Poets & Musicians* (Midleton, 1974).

Costello, C., *Botany Bay The Story of the Convicts transported from Ireland to Australia 1791-1853* (Cork, 1987).

Cowman, D., ed., *The Famine in Waterford 1845-1850 Teacht na bprátaí dubha* (Dungarvan & Dublin, 1995).

Culhane, T.F., *Home Thoughts from Abroad The Australian Letters of Thomas F. Culhane* (Glin, 1998).

Cullen, J.H., *Young Ireland in Exile The Story of the Men of '48 in Tasmania* (Dublin, 1928).

Cullen, L.M., *The Emergence of Modern Ireland 1600-1900* (London, 1981).

Cyclopedia of Tasmania, vol. I (Hobart, 1990).

Davis, R., *The Young Ireland Movement* (Dublin, 1987).

_____, *William Smith O'Brien: Ireland – 1848 – Tasmania* (Dublin, 1989).

_____, 'Patrick O'Donohoe: Outcast of the Exiles' in B. Reece ed., *Exiles from Erin Convict Lives in Ireland and Australia* (Dublin, 1991) pp. 246-83.

_____, 'Unpublicised Young Ireland Prisoners in Van Diemen's Land', *Tasmanian Historical Research Association Papers & Proceedings,* vol. 38, nos. 3 & 4 (December 1991), pp. 131-7.

_____, ed., *'To Solitude Consigned' The Tasmanian Journal of William Smith O'Brien 1849-1853* (Sydney, 1995).

_____, *Revolutionary Imperialist William Smith O'Brien 1803-1864* (Dublin & Sydney, 1998).

De Courcy Ireland, J., 'Fenianism and Naval Affairs', in *Irish Sword,* vol. VIII, no. 30 (Summer 1967), pp. 10-22.

Denieffe, J., *A Personal Narrative of the Irish Revolutionary Brotherhood,* reprint, (Shannon, 1969).

De Quincy, E., *The History of Mount Wellington A Tasmanian Sketchbook* (Hobart, 1987).

Devoy, J., *Recollections of an Irish Rebel* (New York, 1929).

Dictionary of Canadian Biography 1871-1880, vol X (Toronto, 1972).

Dictionary of National Biography, Twentieth Century 1901-1911 (Oxford, 1989 ed).

Doheny, M., *The Felon's Track* (Dublin, 1951).

Donnelly, J., *The Land and People of Nineteenth Century Cork, The Rural Economy and the Land Question* (London, 1973).

Eldershaw, P.R., *Guide to the Public Records of Tasmania Section Three Convict Department* (Hobart, 1965).

Fenton, J., *Bush Life in Tasmania 50 Years Ago* (Launceston, 1991).

Field Officer, A, *Bermuda, A Colony, a Fortress, and a Prison: or Eighteen Months in the Somers' Islands* (London, 1857).

Fitzgerald, J., *Legends, Ballads and Songs of the Lee* (Cork, 1862).

Fitzpatrick, D., *Oceans of Consolation Personal Accounts of Irish Migration to Australia* (Cork, 1994).

Flanagan, T., *The Tenants of Time* (London & New York, 1988).

Fraher, W., Sheridan, B., Ó Loinsigh, S. & Whelan, W., *Desperate Haven, The Poorhouse, Famine & Aftermath in Dungarvan Union* (Midleton, 1995).

Fogarty, L., *James Fintan Lalor Patriot & Political Essayist (1807-1849)* (Dublin, 1921).

Grassby, A. & Hill, M., *Six Australian Battlefields* (North Ryde N.S.W., 1988).

Hughes, R., *The Fatal Shore* (London, 1988).

Johnson, W.B., *The English Prison Hulks*, rev. edition (Chichester, 1970).

Kee, R., *The Most Distressful Country The Green Flag Vol 1* (London, 1989).

Kenealy, A., *Memoirs of Edward Vaughan Kenealy* (London, 1908).

Keneally, T., *The Great Shame A Story of the Irish in the Old World and the New* (London, 1998).

Kiely M.B., *The Connerys The Making of a Waterford Legend* (Dublin, 1994).

_____, *The End of Old Ireland The Failed Revolution of 1849*, lecture (Cappoquin, 1995).

Kiely, M.B. & Nolan, W., 'Politics Land and Rural Conflict in County Waterford c.1830-1845 in Nolan, W., & Power, T.P. eds., *Waterford History & Society* (Dublin, 1992).

Kiernan, T.J., *The Irish Exiles in Australia* (Melbourne, 1954).

Kogan, R., *Brunswick The Story of an American Company The First 150 Years* (Lake Forest, Illinois, 1995).

Lee, J.J., *The Modernisation of Irish Society 1848-1918* (Dublin, 1973).

_____, *Ireland 1912-1985 Politics and Society* (Cambridge, 1989).

_____, 'Remember Ballingarry', *Sunday Tribune,* 26 July 1998.

Lobozza, C., *Stamford Connecticut Pictures from the Past* (Stamford, 1970).

Lord, R., *Impression Bay Convict Probation Station to Civilian Quarantine Station* (Taroona Tas., 1992)

Louisiana Newspapers 1794-1940 (Louisiana State University, 1941).

McCarthy, P., 'James Francis Xavier O'Brien (1828-1905): Dungarvan-born Fenian', in *Decies,* no. 54 (1998), pp. 107-38

Mac Fhinn, P.E., *An tAthair Micheál P. Ó hIceadh*a (Baile Átha Cliath, 1974).

MacManus, M.J., ed., *Thomas Davis and Young Ireland* (Dublin, 1945).

McMullen, A., 'Timber and Sawmilling', *Huon and Derwent Times,* Huon Centenary Settlement (December 1936).

Maher, J., *Chief of the Comeraghs* (Mullinahone, 1957).

Maher, M., *The Devil's Card* (Dingle, 1992).

Mitchel, J., *Jail Journal or Five Years in British Prisons* (New York, 1868).

Molony, J., *Eureka* (Ringwood Vic., 1989).

_____, *A Soul Came into Ireland Thomas Davis 1814-1845* (Dublin, 1995).

Mokyr, J., *Why Ireland Starved A Quantitive and Analytical History of the Irish Economy 1800-1850* (London, 1985).

Moody, T.W. & Martin F.A., *The Course of Irish History* (Cork, 1984).

Moore, T., *The Poetical Works of Thomas Moore* (London, 1854).

Murphy, J.A., *The College A History of Queen's/University College Cork, 1845-1995* (Cork, 1995).

Murphy, S. & S., *The Comeraghs Famine Eviction and Revolution* (Kilmacthomas, 1996).

Murray, K.A. & McNeill, D.B., *The Great Southern & Western Railway* (Dublin, 1976).

Neeson, E., *The Civil War 1922-23,* 2nd ed., (Dublin, 1989).

Nicholas, S., ed., *Convict Workers Reinterpreting Australia's Past* (Cambridge, 1988).

Ní Mhuirí N., 'Teacht na bhFinin go h-Eilvic 1867', i Breathnach, E. ed, *History Lore & Legend through the eyes of the Young* (Waterford, 1987), lcha. 52-3.

Nolan, W., & Power, T.P., *Waterford: History & Society* (Dublin, 1992).

Ó Caoimh, S., *An Sléibhteánach* (Maigh Nuad, 1989).

O'Conner, R., *Jenny Mitchel Young Irelander* (Dublin & Tuscon, 1988).

Ó Cathaoir, B., 'John O'Mahony 1815-1877, *Capuchin Annual* (1977), pp. 180-93.

O'D., D.J., 'Joseph Brenan', *The Irish Book Lover,* vol. V (June 1914), pp. 189-91.

O'Donnell, L., 'Our Irish Heritage', *Derwent Valley Gazette,* 1 & 8 May 1996.

O'Donoghue, F., *No Other Law* (Dublin, 1954).

O'Farrell, P., *The Irish in Australia* (Kensington N.S.W., 1987).

Ó Grada, C., *An Drochshaol Béaloideas agus Amhráin* (Baile Átha Cliath, 1995).

Ó hUiginn, B., 'Herald of the Fenians A Forgotten Meathman', in *Wolfe Tone Annual* (1940), pp. 58-9.

O'Leary, F.X.,'The Black Christmas A Fragment of West Waterford History', *Cork Holly Bough* (1956), pp. 17, 33.

Ó Lúing, S., *John Devoy* (Baile Átha Cliath, 1961).

_____, *The Catalpa Rescue (Reissue of Freemantle Mission)* (Dublin, 1985).

O'Mahony, J., ed., *Foras Feasa ar Eirinn* (New York, 1857).

Ó Mathúna, D., 'Banfhile ó Chorcaigh Mary an Nation', *Agus,* lml. XXX (Deireadh Fomhár 1990), lcha. 20-22.

_____, 'The Vision and Sacrafice of John O Mahony, in *Íris Muintir Mhathghamhna The O'Mahony Journal,* vols. 7 & 8, Summer (1978), pp. 30-4.

Ó Néill, T.P., 'Fintan Lalor and the 1849 Movement', *An Cosantóir,* vol. X, no. 4, April 1950, pp. 173-79.

_____, *Fiontán Ó Leathlobhair* (Baile Átha Cliath, 1962).

O' Shaughessny, P., ed., *The Gardens of Hell John Mitchel in Van Diemen's Land 1850-1853* (Kenthurst N.S.W., 1988).

O'Sullivan, T.F., *The Young Irelanders,* 2nd ed., Tralee, 1945.

O'Toole, L.M.,'The Women Writers of the Nation', in McManus, M.J., ed., *Thomas Davis and Young Ireland* (Dublin, 1945) pp. 119-22.

Ó Tuathaigh, G., *Ireland Before the Famine 1798-1848* (Dublin, 1972).

Pink, K.G., *And Wealth for Toil A History of North-West and Western Tasmania 1825-1900* (Burnie Tas., 1990).

_____, *Through Hell's Gates A History of Strahan and Macquarie Harbour,* 2nd ed (Strahan Tas., 1992).

Pink, K.G. & Abdon, A., *Beyond the Ramparts A Bicentennial History of Circular Head,* Tasmania (Hobart, 1987).

Power, P., *A Compendious History of theUnited Dioceses of Waterford and Lismore* (Cork, 1937).

_____, *Log-Ainmneacha na nDéise The Place-Names of Decies,* 2nd ed (Cork, 1952).

Queensberry, C., *Ireland's Future: An Address to Irishmen* (Maidenhead, 1886).

Reece, B., ed., *Exiles from Erin Convict Lives in Ireland and Australia* (Dublin, 1991).

Rees, J., *Farewell to Famine* (Arklow, 1994).

Robbins, J., *The Miasma Epidemic and Panic in Nineteenth Century Ireland* (Dublin, 1995).

Robson, L., *A Short History of Tasmania* (Melbourne, 1986).

Rudé, G., *Protest and Punishment, The Story of the Social and Political Protestors transported to Australia 1788-1868* (Mebourne, 1978).

Savage, J., *'98 and '48 The Modern Revolutionary History and Literature of Ireland* (New York, 1860).

Senior, H., *The Fenians and Canada* (Toronto, 1978).

Sibeald, T., *A Sketch of the Bermudas or Somers Island* (London, 1851).

Smyme, M.A., *Shipping Arrivals and Departures, Victorian Ports ,* Vol. 2, 1846-1855, (Melbourne, 1987).

Smyth, P.J., *Australasia A Lecture delivered before the Catholic Young Men's Society,* 2nd ed. (Dublin, 1861).

Southerwood, W.J., *Planting a Faith in Tasmania,* The Country Parishes (Hobart, 1977).

_____, *The Convict's Friend (Bishop R.W.Willson)* (George Town Tas., 1989).

Statistics of Van Diemen's Land 1844-1853 (Hobart, 1854).

Sullivan, G., *General Thomas Francis Meagher A Sketch* (Butte Mont., 1905).

Teagasc, *Late Blight & the Potato in Ireland* (Carlow, 1995).

The Nation 1848-1998 Commemorative Re-issue (Killenaule, 1998).

Transactions of the Society of Friends during the Famine in Ireland, reprint (Dublin, 1996).

Tucker, T., *Bermuda Today and Yesterday 1503-1978,* 2nd ed., (London & Bermuda, 1978).

Vaughan, P., *The Last Forge in Lismore* (Dublin, 1994).

Wannan, B., ed., *The Wearing of the Green: The Lore, Literature, Legend and Balladry of the Irish in Australia* (Melbourne, 1965).

Wapping History Group, *'Down Wapping' Hobart's vanished Wapping and Old Wharf Districts* (Hobart, 1988).

Whitaker, A., *Unfinished Revolution United Irishmen in New South Wales 1800-1810* (Sydney, 1994).

Williams, J., *Ordered to the Island Irish Convicts and Van Diemen's Land* (Sydney, 1994).

Woodham-Smith, C., *The Great Hunger Ireland 1845-1849* (London, 1987).

Young Ireland Rising Commemoration 1848-1998 (Killenaule, 1998).

Zuill, W.S., *The Story of Bermuda and her People,* 2nd ed., (London, 1983).

4. Unpublished Works

Chamberlain, S., The Hobart Whaling Industry 1830-1890 Phd. Thesis La Trobe University 1988.

McCarthy, T., Inscriptions from Old Affane Cemetery.

Mac Lochlainn, A., William Paul Dowling Letters of a Transported Felon, lecture at Ninth Irish-Australian History Conference, Galway 1997.

Taylor, J. & Smyth, J., A Dictionary of Tasmanian Place Names, work in progress, in Tasmanian Library 1993.

INDEX

143

California, 55
Callaghan, Martin, 63, 65
Camphire, 19, 81
Campobello Island, 88
Canaan, 15
Canada, 88, 90, 129
Cane, Dr. Robert, 13
Cappoquin, 1, 16, 18-19, 21-8, 36-8, 40-1, 44-7, 50, 53, 56-7, 59, 62, 66, 81, 83, 101-3, 110, 128-9
Carrickbeg, 27, 38, 41, 50, 62-3, 66
Carrick-on-Suir, 2, 16, 38-9, 50, 63, 65, 67, 83
Casey, James 27, 58
Cascades, 54-5, 58, 63
Cashel, 16, 21-2
Cashel & Emly Diocese, 9
Cash, Martin, 44
Cashman, Patrick, 27
Castle Forbes Bay, 55
Castle Eden, 41
Castle Hill, 84
Catalpa, 74
Cavan, 62
Cavanagh, Michael, 1, 23-4, 87-8, 96-101, 108-9
Ceitinn, SeathrÊn, 85
Champlain, Lake, 38
Chartists, 4, 11, 13, 45, 69, 70, 84, 94
Cincinnatti, 24
Circular Head, 56
Citizen, 4
Clarendon, Lord, 11, 27, 39, 65, 67-8, 128
Clarke, John, 129
Clongowes Wood, 58

Clonmel, 13, 16, 21-2, 27, 39, 58, 71, 96
Clonoulty, 21
Clontarf, 5
Clare, 16
Cleary, Catherine, 59-60
Clonea DÎiseach, 26
Clonea Paorach, 83
Clonocogaile, 19
Collender, Hugh, 23, 24-6
Colonial Office, 38
Colonial Times and Tasmanian, 45
Comeragh mts., 4, 18
Connacht, 81, 103
Connecticut, 24
Connell, John, 128
Connerys, The, 81
Cork, 5, 8, 11, 13-4, 16, 22, 25, 57, 70, 96, 107, 129
Cork Examiner, 18, 22, 46
Cornelian Bay Cemetery, 55 ,69, 71
Coromandel, 32, 37
Corra Linn, 59
Cove, 14, 40
Cove Hill, 26
Craughwell, 76
Crimea, 84
Cronin, James, 40
Cronin, Thomas, 40
Crotty, James 28, 32, 40-1, 102
Cruachïn Paorach, 4
Crumlin Road Gaol, 11
Cruttenden, Thomas 68
Cullen, Paul, 81
Cunningham, Philip, 96
Curragh, The, 16
Cygnet, 53, 75

Daly, Cornelius, 27

Dante, 11
Darien, 24
Davis, Richard, 12
Dease, Mr., 67-8
Dee, John, 63
De h'de, Dubhglas, 101
Denison, Sir William, 44-5, 53
De Valera, îamonn, 97
Devoy, John, 74, 97
Doheny, Michael, 10, 18, 70, 97
Dolphin's Barn, 12
Donegal Bay, 90
Donohoe, James, 21, 25, 27, 102, 110
Donohoe, John, 25, 27-8, 32-3, 36, 38, 40-1, 102
Donohoe, Margaret, 27-8
Donohoe, Michael, 27-8, 36
Donovan, Peter, 55
Donovan, Thomas, 27, 53-5, 75, 94
Dowling, William Paul, 45-6, 50, 69-72
Downing, Mary Ellen, 11, 22-3, 107-8
Doyle, William, 32, 35-6, 46, 62
Dromedary, 32, 37
Drumcondra, 52
Drumgallon, 88
Drummond, Thomas, 33
Drumroe, 28
Dry, Richard, 72
Dwyer, Hanora, 52-3, 75
Dwyer, James, 110
Dwyer, William, 75
Dublin, 5, 11-14, 28, 45, 52, 62, 72, 80, 83-4, 86, 108
Dublin Castle, 9, 11, 14, 28, 35, 65, 87, 94
Dublin Evening Post, 46

Duffy, Charles Gavan, 12, 47, 92
Dungarvan, 4, 8, 16, 21, 23, 25-6, 30, 46, 59, 81, 86, 96
Dutch East Indies, 83
Dysentery, 38

East India Company, 56, 129
Elliot, Governor, 32, 35, 40
Elphin Station, 72
Enfield, 85
England, 5, 8, 48, 66
Erin's Hope, 88, 108
Eureka Stockade, 84

Fahey, Bridget, 27
Fahy, Hanora, 54
Faithlegg, 47
Famine, The, 1, 80, 96
Farrenrory, 2, 4, 110
Fay, Thomas, 45, 50, 69-71
Ferns Diocese, 9
Figlash, 32, 39
Firies, 52
Fitzgerald, John, 106-7
Fitzpatrick, Richard, 16
Flavahan, Maurice, 27
Flying Columns, 16
Fogarty, Anne, 57
Fogarty, Fr. Michael, 83
Fontaine, 81
Foran, Bishop Nicholas, 25, 65
France, 45, 84, 88
Franklin Tas., 50, 52-3, 55, 67
Franklin Vt., 90
Freeman's Journal, 46
French Government, 8
Fulham, Bernard, 12

Galtee foothills, 35, 103
Galway, City, 5

O'Brien, William Smith, 2,4, 8-10,
    13, 16, 46, 48, 57-8, 67,
    70-1, 83, 94, 96
Observer, 46
~ Caoimh, Sîamus, 1, 21
~ Caoimh, Sîan, 19, 24
O'Connell, Daniel,5-9, 80, 87, 92
O'Connell, John, 8
O'Connor, Feargus, 11
O'Connor, Fr. Michael, 81
O'Doherty, Kevin Izod, 13, 46, 48,
    58, 83
O'Donohoe, Edward, 13
O'Donohoe, Patrick, 10, 13, 48, 57
O'Donovan Rossa, Jer., 87, 90
O'Gorman, Richard Jr., 10
~ Hailli, Micheïl, 19, 24
~ hUiginn, Brian, 97
Ohio, 24
Old Bailey, 13, 70, 72
Olden, Subcon., 128
O'Leary, John, 11,13, 21-3, 87-88,
    92
Omaha, 106
O'Mahony, John, 2, 4, 12, 23, 67,
    84-90, 94, 96-7, 103
O'Meagher, Henry E.F., 47, 51
O'Neill, John, 88, 90
Ontario,88
O'Rourke, Patrick M., 129
Ossory Diocese, 9
Owens, James, 19, 25, 27, 102,
    110, 128

Pacific Ocean, 66
Paor, îamonn, 96
Paris, 8, 12, 46
Pearl, 40
Peel, Sir Robert, 5
Pembina, 90

Pennefather, Judge, 60
Pentonville, 88
Pernambuco, 47
Pestonjee Bomanjee, 35
Phoenix Park, 16
Picton River, 53
Pipers River, 62
Pitcairn Islanders, 67
Port Arthur, 53. 60
Port Davey, 53
Portland, 88
Portlaw, 2, 22-3, 32, 35-6, 46, 50,
    62-3, 65-6, 110
Potatoes, 7, 32
Poulacapple, 103
Powell, Thomas, 69
Power, Catherine, 27
Power, Gow, 29
Price, Governor, 66
Probation System, 44
Prossers Plains, 68

Quebec, 128
Queen's Colleges, 5, 14, 80
Queenstown Ire., 14, 28, 39, 62,
    66-7, 90
Quinlan, William, 35

Rathclarish, 39
Rathgormack, 2, 29, 63, 83, 110
Rathmines, 12
Ream's Station, 87
Redington, Sir Thomas, 26-7, 128-
    9
Red River Valley, 90
Reeves, Isaac G., 57
Regan, Jeanie, 58, 72
Regan, John, 57-8
Reilly, Thomas Devin, 4, 10
Reynolds, Dr. Lawrence, 71

* Please also see Appendices 3 &
5 which are in alphabetical order.